VOLUME 14 • ISSUE 2 • FALL 2022

GREAT COMMISSION
RESEARCH JOURNAL

Published by the Great Commission Research Network

© 2022 Great Commission Research Network

Published by the Great Commission Research Network (GCRN)
GCRN's Registered Agent: Corporation Service Company
7716 Old Canton Road, Suite C
Madison, MS 39110

www.greatcommissionresearch.com

Printed in the United States of America by Martel Press, Claremont, CA

Correspondence: 695 E. Bougainvillea St., Azusa, CA 91702 USA

THE PURPOSE of the *Great Commission Research Journal* is to communicate recent thinking and research related to effective church growth and evangelism.

THE JOURNAL The *Great Commission Research Journal* (formerly, *The Journal of the American Society for Church Growth*) is published semi-annually, Fall and Spring. It is indexed in *Christian Periodical Index* and the *Atla Religion Database*.

ISSN 1947-5837 (print)
ISSN 2638-9983 (online)
ISBN 978-1-7377520-1-1

THE OPINIONS AND CONCLUSIONS published in the Great Commission Research Journal are solely those of the individual authors and do not necessarily represent the position of the Great Commission Research Network.

GENERAL EDITOR:
David R. Dunaetz, ddunaetz@apu.edu
Azusa Pacific University, California, USA
ASSISTANT EDITOR:
Hannah Jung, hannahtrinity1@gmail.com
Azusa Pacific University, California, USA
BOOK REVIEW EDITOR:
Kenneth Nehrbass, krnehrbass@liberty.edu
Liberty University, Virginia, USA
EDITORIAL BOARD MEMBERS:
Moses Audi, Baptist Theological Seminary, Kaduna, Nigeria
Alan McMahan, Biola University, California, USA
Brent Burdick, Gordon Conwell Theological Seminary, North Carolina, USA

PAST EDITORS:	John Vaughan	1991-1995
	Gary L. McIntosh	1996-2008
	Alan McMahan	2009-2018
	Mike Morris	2018-2020

CONTENTS

GREAT COMMISSION
RESEARCH JOURNAL
2022, Vol. 14(2) 5-17

Church-Based Research: Using Theories, Concepts, and Operationalizations

David R. Dunaetz, Editor
Azusa Pacific University

Abstract

Church-based research requires working with abstract concepts ranging from sin to sanctification. Theories, concepts, and operationalizations allow us to work with these abstractions. Theories are sets of statements describing how specific concepts relate to each other. Concepts are broad ideas that exist in our thinking that can be used to describe phenomena, both within and exterior to the church. If we measure the concepts in our theories among multiple people, we can determine to what degree the relationships in our theories are true or discover under what conditions they are true. Sometimes concepts can be measured directly; other times they must be measured indirectly. Operationalizations are the specific processes used for measuring each of the concepts. As we test and refine our theories, we can more effectively accomplish the ministries to which we are called.

Jesus was born, lived, died, and rose again. The foundation of the gospel lies in observable, concrete phenomena. But many very abstract concepts and phenomena are associated with what he did: faith, repentance, the new birth, spiritual growth, holiness, and love. One of the goals of church-based research is to understand how these abstract concepts and phenomena are related to other abstract ideas as well as how they are related to more concrete phenomena. These phenomena are not limited to what Jesus did as recorded in the gospels, but also include the mundane such as phenomena related to parking lots, video projectors, and social media. Sometimes we want to know what phenomena exist in our church (e.g., what do people do in my church's small groups?). Other times we want to know how common a specific phenomenon is in a group of churches (e.g., how many churches in our denomination have Instagram accounts?). Even more important is discovering relationships between these phenomena (How, and under what conditions, can Instagram content influence a church's small groups?)

Some, if not most, of the questions to which we would like answers require research. We need to go collect data and make conclusions. But how to do so is not obvious, especially for more complex problems where many factors come into play. Improperly designed ministry-focused research might produce a mishmash of information that does not lend itself to credible answers, wasting everyone's time and resources, or even worse, leading us to believe something that is not true, something that makes our disciple making ministry less effective, rather than more effective. To prevent this from happening, both concrete and abstract phenomena need to be examined appropriately. Theories, concepts, and operationalizations are all used to do this. High-quality research will focus on concepts that fit together in a theory and can be measured by using operationalizations.

Theories

Theories are found at the top level of abstraction in research. A theory can be defined as a set of statements describing some specific concepts and how they relate to each other (Morling, 2021; Sutton & Staw, 1995). A theory is typically presented in some convenient way that summarizes what the author believes to be true about the concepts and how they relate (Crano et al., 2015). A theory does not try to describe every possible phenomenon that is associated with the chosen concepts, but rather it describes general principles of how these concepts relate to each other. The purpose of a theory is to enable decisions to be made concerning the related concepts and to guide our observations of experience in applied, real-life settings. For Christian workers concerned with disciple making, theology is usually the most familiar use of theory.

Theology is theory in that it is typically a set of statements about God, including a description of his nature, what he desires, and how he interacts with the world. A theology is typically based on divine (or special) revelation (e.g., the Bible), applied to a more or less general context through rational argument. Different theologies develop (e.g., Reformed, Arminian, Restorationist, and Pentecostal) because of differences in prioritization concerning the biblical texts or the use of different rational arguments to connect the various concepts together.

In addition to theology, many other theories have been developed that a Christian worker may encounter. Some theories are not especially relevant to disciple making (e.g., the theory of relativity, which is only relevant at astronomical distances or extremely high speeds, quantum theory, which is only relevant on the atomic and subatomic levels, or any of myriads of scientific theories that are only marginally relevant to human behavior). Some theories are relevant to the degree that they help us understand culture or direct our apologetics to respond to people's needs (e.g., evolution and critical race theory). However, other theories, especially those that describe human behavior are very relevant to disciple making and other church-based ministries.

An example of a secular theory that is relevant to disciple-making, taken from the field of social psychology, is the broaden-and-build theory (Fredrickson, 2001, 2003) which states that positive emotions enable a person to better explore new ideas and take risks. Experiencing positive emotions (like joy, peace, awe, love, or gratitude) usually indicates that we are in a safe psychological space. This allows us to consider new information and ideas (rather than be on the defensive, where we often become closed to new ideas). This enables us to learn, that is, to broaden our knowledge base and build upon it. For disciple makers, this is an important phenomenon since Jesus said that one of our main responsibilities is to teach people "to obey everything I have commanded you" (Matt. 28:20). This means that creating an atmosphere that generates positive emotions, makes it more likely that, when we teach this material, people will be ready to reflect on it and incorporate it into their lives as they broaden their knowledge of what God desires of and for them and build their capacity to respond in Christ-like ways to the various situations that they encounter as they go through life. Creating positive emotions does not mean that we need to limit our teaching to simple, non-offensive ideas presented with jokes and lighthearted stories. Rather, we can present all the difficult teachings of Jesus, ranging from counting the cost of discipleship to complex theological truths to counter-cultural expectations for behavior in families and in the church, if we present it in a way that demonstrates its benefits, that is, if we can show that it is advantageous to follow Christ whole-heartedly compared to the alternatives. Presenting Christ's teachings in this way will create the targeted positive emotions, although it requires much preparatory work.

Another example of a secular theory relevant to disciple making is inoculation theory (Compton, 2013; McGuire, 1961) which states that people can be inoculated against arguments attacking what they believe. To inoculate people against such influence, they need to be introduced to arguments against their beliefs and how to respond to these arguments. These responses are called counterarguments and need to be presented before the argument against one's beliefs is presented by someone who does not share these beliefs. Extensive empirical evidence has demonstrated that the presentation of counterarguments protects people's beliefs even when later faced with strong evidence against what they believe (Banas & Rains, 2010). In a period when abandoning the faith, often called deconversion (Streib, 2021), is becoming more common, the relevance of this theory is clear. Simply explaining to people that God exists and what the Bible says may not be sufficient when they are bombarded with arguments on the internet against the existence of God, Christianity, and the veracity of the Bible (e.g., reddit.com/r/atheism). People, especially youth, need to hear Christian leaders address the arguments that they will hear from their peers and online. If they do not, they can assume that the arguments against God and Christianity are valid because their pastors and teachers have never presented evidence against them. If they cannot come up with counterarguments, their faith may be shaken (Dunaetz, 2016). A meta-analysis of over 50 studies (Banas & Rains, 2010) found that counterarguments provided maximum immunity for about two weeks before people became more susceptible to arguments against their beliefs. This would mean that Christians susceptible to questioning their faith should be exposed to counterarguments to what atheists are arguing at least twice a month.

These are just two examples of secular theories that are relevant to disciple making. Countless others could be included. Although theology (at least evangelical theology) is primarily developed through interacting with biblical texts (special revelation), theories focusing on how humans interact, both with each other and with God, can be based on observation (general revelation). However, because there is so much variety in human behavior, many observations need to be made before theories can be generated and tested (e.g., Nehrbass, 2022, in this issue for how a a theory can be generated).

Theories should never be considered complete or unchangeable. They are not complete because, by definition, they only seek to explain relationships between several (typically only a few) concepts. For example, many churches and parachurch organizations emphasize training in personal evangelism so that more people come to know the Lord. The underlying theory of programs such as Evangelism Explosion in its original form (Kennedy, 1970) describes how some people, when confronted with the gospel, will make decisions to follow the Lord. Therefore, Christians should be trained in how to share their faith accurately and concisely with everyone they meet. This theory links training in personal evangelism, communicating the gospel, and individual conversions. It does not claim to be a complete theory of evangelism, that is, it does not claim to describe how other forms of evangelism work, all the ways that Christians can be trained, or how most people actually come to know the Lord. It simply describes how training in personal evangelism can lead more people to Christ.

Theories are not static because they evolve both with additional research and for social reasons. Additional research can provide a better description of how the phenomena described in the theory relate to each other (see Hong & Botner, 2022, in this issue for how competing notions of humility relate to following Christ.). Additional research may also introduce new concepts and show how they relate to the concepts described in existing theory. Typically, advances in theory are relatively small (See Scheuermann, 2022, for a small but important advancement in apologetics), but sometimes there are major innovations that seem to have the potential to change everything (e.g. saturation evangelism where the gospel is presented to people through modern technological and commercial means rather than through individuals). As our experience with the innovation grows, it may create a radically different way of viewing the phenomenon (a paradigm shift; Kuhn, 1962), or more likely, will eventually be incorporated into our existing theories (e.g., saturation evangelism is one way to present the gospel among others and sometimes opens doors for a personal presentation of the gospel).

Theories can also evolve for social reasons (Crano et al., 2015). As technologies and cultures change, new research questions arise such as "How can social media be used for evangelism?" (Bocala-Wiedemann, 2022; Teasdale, 2022, in this issue) or "How is the use of technology related to stress in church planting?" (Dunaetz, 2022). As these research questions are answered, our theories of evangelism and church planting evolve little by little. Theories can also evolve because of trends, the ebb and flow of popular personalities or researchers, and cultural forces which influence what people pay attention to. When cultural forces make a biblical faith more attractive, our evangelism theories will focus on growth (e.g., McGavran & Wagner, 1990), and when cultural forces make a biblical faith less attractive, evangelicals may be tempted to downplay the importance of evangelism and focus on social actions and theories that are more culturally attractive.

Concepts

Theories explain how concepts relate to each other. Concepts are broad ideas that exist in our thinking that can be used to describe phenomena. Some concepts are observable and even measurable. By collecting data related to the concepts in our theory, we can test to what degree or under what conditions the various parts of the theory are true.

Take, for example, social identity theory (Hogg, 2006; Turner, 1982) which states that our beliefs about ourselves (our identity) are influenced by the groups to which we belong, and our perception of others is influenced by the groups to which they belong. In contrast to our personal identity (which is based on our traits and abilities, especially those which make us different from others), our social identity is based on the perceived typical traits of members of the groups to which we belong (Stets & Burke, 2000). For example, my personal identity is strongly influenced by my former career as a church planter and by how God opened the doors for me to become a professor of organizational psychology. My social identity includes being an evangelical Christian, a faculty member at Azusa Pacific University, a member of Purpose Church in Pomona, California, and a white Gen X American with a secular Judeo-Christian heritage.

Among other things, social identity theory describes that when group membership is salient (e.g., emphasized by others or in our own thinking), several phenomena tend to occur. One is ingroup favoritism which causes us to interpret ambiguous information in a way that makes members of our ingroup look better. Another phenomenon is outgroup derogation which causes us to interpret ambiguous information in a way that makes members of our outgroups look worse. One of the underlying mechanisms which cause these phenomena is our desire to maintain our self-esteem; we are motivated to view ourselves as better than others (Balliet et al., 2014; Branscombe & Wann, 1994). This desire to see ourselves as better than others, sometimes even better than God, is a human problem that goes back to the Garden of Eden (Genesis 3:1-13).

From a theological perspective, social identity theory partially explains why Paul's statement in Colossians 3:11 describing the church is so important, "Here there is no Gentile or Jew, circumcised or uncircumcised, barbarian, Scythian, slave or free, but Christ is all, and is in all" (NIV). Whereas emphasizing demographic group memberships leads to ingroup favoritism and outgroup derogation, emphasizing that following Christ is the central aspect of our identity provides a basis for true reconciliation and unity with believers of other demographics (cf. Eph. 2:11-12, Gal. 3:26-29).

Returning to the notion of concepts, we see that social identity theory describes the relationships between various concepts. We have *identity*, people's beliefs about who they are, *group membership*, the idea that a person can identify as belonging to various groups defined by demographics, beliefs, values, interests, or virtually anything else, *ingroup*, people with whom we share a salient group membership, *outgroups*, groups of individuals of which we are not a member, *favoritism*, adjusting our thinking and actions to benefit some people more than others, and *derogation*, adjusting our thinking and actions (especially our speech) to provide evidence that some people are less valuable. These concepts are all linked in statements describing their relationship to each other, making social identity theory a theory, and not just a set of concepts.

Typically, concepts described in theories can vary for different people, different groups, or different situations, and can thus be considered variables. In social identity theory, identity varies among individuals, just as the group membership varies among individuals. Similarly, the degree to which people practice ingroup favoritism and outgroup derogation varies by individual and it also varies by circumstance. When there is variation in human behavior as in these examples, it is typically *normally distributed*, that is, there is a normal or average amount of behavior displayed by humans; most humans' behavior is fairly close to the average, but there are a few who display the behavior much more than others and a few who display much less of the behavior.

Because human behavior varies so much, it is often difficult to determine if one group differs from another group, on average, for a given concept or variable. For example, we might want to know if people are more committed to their church in one congregation than in another. Without collecting data, it would be hard to make a call. This is especially true because variation within groups is almost always greater than the variation between groups. For example, both congregations that interest us will have people who have very high commitment and people who have low commitment, that is, there is a lot of variation within each congregation. It is likely that the difference between the average level of commitment of the two congregations (the variation between churches) is much smaller than the variation within the congregations. Typically, we use inferential statistics (i.e., not just descriptive statistics that describe each variable separately) to test the idea, or hypothesis, that one congregation has a higher level of commitment than the other by collecting a sample from each and making inferences based on what we know about normally distributed variables (like church commitment).

Some concepts, or variables, are easily observable and can be measured in a very straightforward manner. If measuring the variable is more or less objective, such as a person's age, sex, city of residence, or educational level, a single question on a survey might be enough to measure it. If we are measuring a complex phenomenon, several questions might be necessary to capture its various aspects. The difficulty of measurement also depends on the level of analysis being used in the study: Are we collecting data on individuals, small groups, churches, or denominations? Generally, getting data from smaller units of analysis is easier than getting it from larger ones. It is much easier to collect data from 300 individuals than it is from 300 small groups, 300 churches, and especially from 300 denominations.

Any time we wish to collect data on a concept, it is important to first clearly define what we want to measure. Even with relatively objective measures, especially as the unit of analysis grows, we need to be as clear as possible to reduce the error in our data. For example, if the unit of analysis is the church, we could ask the question "What was the average attendance of the church over the last year?" However, it is not clear what "average attendance" means. Is it the average number of people that come to the campus each week? Is it the average total attendance of the worship services on Sundays? Is it the average of the sum of the number of people in all the meetings that a church has on a Sunday morning (thus double counting people who attend Sunday School and the worship service)? Does it have to be based on data from 52 weeks, or is two weeks' worth of data enough? There is no right answer, but to collect meaningful data we need to be clear as possible concerning what we would like churches to count.

Some concepts that we would like to measure to test our theories (or hypotheses, if we are only testing parts of a theory) are not directly observable. Our thoughts, feelings, beliefs, values, and attitudes are not directly measurable because they exist in our heads and are only available subjectively. However, researchers have developed quite reliable ways of measuring such mental phenomena (Crano et al., 2015; Katz, 1960). In these cases, the concepts or variables are called *constructs* because natural measures of them do not exist but need to be constructed by using indirect measures (Crano et al., 2015; Edwards & Bagozzi, 2000), typically by asking someone to indicate how much they agree with a series of statements related to the construct.

Constructs that could be of interest in church-based research include church commitment (Covarrubias et al., 2021), personality traits of leaders such as extraversion, humility, and conscientiousness (Barrick & Mount, 1991; Lee & Ashton, 2004), characteristics of small group Bible studies (Hartwig et al., 2020), pastoral attitudes toward various ministries (Dunaetz & Priddy, 2014), and any of a myriad of other phenomena that might reflect or influence people's thoughts, feelings, and behaviors in churches.

When measuring any variable, clear definitions need to be the starting point. We have seen this previously with church size, but it is equally important for psychological constructs which cannot be measured directly. For example, church commitment can be defined in many different ways. Since the church is the body of Christ, one could define it as one's commitment to the person of Christ. But churches are also human organizations, so definitions focusing on the organizational side of commitment could be used instead (Allen & Meyer, 1990; Meyer & Allen, 1991). Three definitions of organizational commitment are affective organizational commitment (how much a person is emotionally attached to an organization), normative organizational commitment (the degree to which a person believes he or she has a moral duty to stay in an organization), and continuance organizational commitment (the fear of loss that comes from leaving an organization). All four types of commitment are very important because they influence people's thoughts, feelings, and behaviors when they participate in church activities and ministries. When conducting a study, we would need to choose one definition to study, or perhaps we could choose several and treat them as different dimensions of commitment to see how they influence people differently.

Once we have a clear definition of what we want to study, we can develop a way to measure it. This is known as the *operationalization* of a concept or construct and involves clarifying the procedures (e.g., counting church attendees) or determining the instruments (e.g., sets of survey items) that we will use. Once we have chosen operationalizations for the concepts in our theories or hypotheses, we can begin collecting and compiling data from individuals, groups, churches, or whatever else we are studying.

Operationalizations

Good operationalizations of the concepts we want to measure lay at the heart of science. Independent researchers should be able to measure a concept in the same individual and get approximately the same result (Crano et al., 2015). Operationalizations should be both valid and reliable. An operationalization is valid to the degree that we measure the true value of whatever we have defined. Note that most scientists who hold to the belief that we can measure real phenomena more or less accurately are working from a postpositivist perspective (Kuhn, 1962; Popper, 1959). This is the idea that objective reality exists, but because of human biases, imperfections, and other limitations, we may not be able to measure it accurately. From a theological perspective, postpositivism is completely compatible with the biblical view of the world which would hold that reality exists, and that God perceives its condition perfectly, while humans who are made in his likeness but are fallen and marred by sin can perceive reality to some degree (by both natural and special revelation), but our perceptions are likely to be less than perfectly accurate.

An operationalization is considered reliable if different researchers can use it to measure the variable or construct and obtain close to the same result. For example, if there are specific instructions on how to count people on Sunday morning (an operationalization), two different researchers should be able to follow the instructions and get the same results. To tell how well they matched up, they could each measure attendance for several Sundays at the same church. A correlation could be calculated to see how well their counts matched. The average of the counts could also be compared to see if one person was systematically counting more people than the other. Furthermore, to determine if an operationalization is reliable, if the measure is administered twice, it should yield the same result in situations where it is reasonable to assume that the underlying phenomenon has not changed. If we are measuring a person's commitment to a church (e.g., Covarrubias et al., 2021), we want an operationalization that does not vary much from week to week. If the person were to complete a survey one week, their commitment score should not vary much from what they would indicate if they were surveyed a week or a month later, apart from extenuating circumstances.

It should be noted that there is no "correct" operationalization for a given concept. For example, God knows our personality. He would not use a 7- or a 10-item survey to determine our level of extraversion. He might not even think in terms of extraversion and introversion. However, if we want to measure people's level of extraversion, we will want to use a validated scale that is known to be reliable. Several such scales exist (John & Srivastava, 1999) but none can be considered the "right" one. As long as it accurately and reliably measures the construct as we have defined it, then we can use any of these. Similarly, there is no single right way to measure church commitment or the average number of people who attend a church. If we can accurately and reliably measure attendance as we have defined it using one of several operationalizations, any of them is fine, as long as we use it consistently.

Conclusion

Theories, concepts, and operationalizations make research possible and are among the tools that help us better understand our world where the Lord has called us to make disciples. Theories provide explanations of how concepts relate to each other. When we operationalize these concepts, we can test our theories to see if they are true and discover specific conditions under which they are true or not. We can test various aspects of our theories by collecting data which allows us to examine specific hypotheses. When we more clearly define concepts and refine our theories, we can become more effective servants of the Lord as we better understand what works and what does not work to help others follow him.

David R. Dunaetz, Editor
ddunaetz@apu.edu

References

Allen, N. J., & Meyer, J. P. (1990). The measurement and antecedents of affective, continuance and normative commitment to the organization. *Journal of Occupational Psychology, 63*(1), 1-18.

Balliet, D., Wu, J., & De Dreu, C. K. W. (2014). Ingroup favoritism in cooperation: A meta-analysis. *Psychological Bulletin, 140*(6), 1556-1581.

Banas, J. A., & Rains, S. A. (2010). A meta-analysis of research on inoculation theory. *Communication Monographs, 77*(3), 281-311.

Barrick, M. R., & Mount, M. K. (1991). The Big Five personality dimensions and job performance: A meta-analysis. *Personnel Psychology, 44*(1), 1-26.

Bocala-Wiedemann, T. J. (2022). Social media as a tool for evangelism among youth and young adults. *Great Commission Research Journal, 14*(1), 19-34.

Branscombe, N. R., & Wann, D. L. (1994). Collective self-esteem consequences of outgroup derogation when a valued social identity is on trial. *European Journal of Social Psychology, 24*(6), 641-657.

Compton, J. (2013). Inoculation theory. In L. Shen & J. P. Dillard (Eds.), *The SAGE handbook of persuasion: Developments in theory and practice* (2nd ed., pp. 220-237).

Covarrubias, A., Dunaetz, D. R., & Dykes, W. (2021). Innovativeness and church commitment: What innovations were most important during the pandemic? *Great Commission Research Journal, 13*(2), 49-70.

Crano, W. D., Brewer, M. B., & Lac, A. (2015). *Principles and methods of social research* (3rd ed.). Routledge.

Dunaetz, D. R. (2016). Missio-logoi and faith: Factors that influence attitude certainty. *Missiology: An International Review, 44*(1), 66-77.

Dunaetz, D. R. (2022). When technology does more bad than good: Technostress in missionary contexts. *Journal of the Evangelical Missiological Society, 2*(1), 112-128.

Dunaetz, D. R., & Priddy, K. E. (2014). Pastoral attitudes that predict numerical Church Growth. *Great Commission Research Journal, 5,* 241-256.

Edwards, J. R., & Bagozzi, R. P. (2000). On the nature and direction of relationships between constructs and measures. *Psychological Methods, 5*(2), 155-174.

Fredrickson, B. L. (2001). The role of positive emotions in positive psychology: The boraden-and-build theory of positive emotions. *American Psychologist, 56*(3), 218-226.

Fredrickson, B. L. (2003). Positive emotions and upward spirals in organizations. In J. E. Dutton, R. E. Quinn, & K. S. Cameron (Eds.), *Positive organizational scholarship* (pp. 163-175). Berrett-Koehler.

Hartwig, R. T., Davis, C. W., & Sniff, J. A. (2020). *Leading small groups that thrive.* Zondervan.

Hogg, M. A. (2006). Social identity theory. In P. J. Burke (Ed.), *Contemporary social psychological theories* (pp. 111-136). Stanford University Press.

Hong, E., & Botner, M. (2022). Competing notions of humility: Why Korean Americans do not need to abandon confucius to get to Christ *Great Commission Research Journal, 14*(2), 19-29.

John, O. P., & Srivastava, S. (1999). The Big-Five trait taxonomy: History, measurement, and theoretical perspectives. In L. A. Pervin & O. P. John (Eds.), *Handbook of personality: Theory and research* (pp. 102-138). Guilford.

Katz, D. (1960). The functional approach to the study of attitudes. *Public Opinion Quarterly, 24,* 163-204.

Kennedy, D. J. (1970). *Evangelism explosion: The Coral Ridge program for lay witness.* Tyndale House Publishers.

Kuhn, T. S. (1962). *The structure of scientific revolutions.* University of Chicago Press.

Lee, K., & Ashton, M. C. (2004). Psychometric properties of the HEXACO personality inventory. *Multivariate Behavioral Research, 39*(2), 329-358.

McGavran, D. A., & Wagner, C. P. (1990). *Understanding church growth* (Third ed.). Eerdmans.

McGuire, W. J. (1961). Resistance to persuasion conferred by active and passive prior refutation of the same and alternative counterarguments. *The Journal of Abnormal and Social Psychology, 63*(2), 326-332.

Meyer, J. P., & Allen, N. J. (1991). A three-component conceptualization of organizational commitment. *Human Resource Management Review, 1,* 61-89.

Morling, B. (2021). *Research methods in psychology* (4th ed.). Norton.

Nehrbass, K. (2022). Not just the sinner's prayer: People's experiences with "stranger-evangelism". *Great Commission Research Journal, 14*(2), 45-64.

Popper, K. (1959). *The logic of scientific discovery.* Routledge.

Scheuermann, R. (2022). Apologetics and disability: Reframing our response to the question of suffering. *Great Commission Research Journal, 14*(2), 85-102.

Stets, J. E., & Burke, P. J. (2000). Identity theory and social identity theory. *Social Psychology Quarterly, 63*(3), 224-237.

Streib, H. (2021). Leaving religion: Deconversion. *Current Opinion in Psychology, 40*, 139-144.

Sutton, R. I., & Staw, B. M. (1995). What theory is not. *Administrative Science Quarterly, 40*(3), 371-384.

Teasdale, M. R. (2022). Forming saints in a digital context. *Great Commission Research Journal, 14*(2), 65-84.

Turner, J. C. (1982). Towards a cognitive redefinition of the group. In H. Tajfel (Ed.), *Social identity and intergroup relations*. Cambridge University Press.

GREAT COMMISSION
RESEARCH JOURNAL
2022, Vol. 14(2) 19-29

Competing Notions of Humility: Why Korean Americans Do Not Need to Abandon Confucius to Get to Christ

Eunice Hong
Cornerstone University
Max Botner
William Jessup University

Abstract

Koreans Americans often go to church not only for religious reasons, but also for social and cultural reasons. Due to the close tie between the Korean immigrant church and cultural traditions, second-generation Korean Americans often struggle with trying to balance Eastern and Western cultural values. In particular, tensions arise for second-generation Korean Americans between competing notions of humility. Such tensions, however, provide opportunities to reflect on the particular nature of Christian humility. This article presents biblical humility as one that is neither the maintenance of cultural traditions nor the personal growth of individual disciples; rather, Christ-shaped, Spirit-filled humility is the cultivation of right relationship with the creator God.

This publication benefited from a fellowship at Biola University's Center for Christian Thought where Eunice served as the pastor-in-residence. The fellowship was made possible through the support of a grant from Templeton Religion Trust.

Attending church is important in the Korean American community, not only for reasons that are religious and spiritual but also social and cultural. Sung Park (1997) states that Korean Christians go to church for four main reasons: fellowship, culture, social service, and social status. Likewise, Jung Oh (2004, p. 126) observes,

> For the first generation the church is both a place of social interaction and cultural identification. After all, they speak the same language and share the same values and customs; and much of their unique cultural behaviour is mutually reinforced in the social contacts provided by the church.

Second-generation Korean Americans, however, have a different relationship with the church. That is, in contrast to their parents, who attend the KM (Korean Ministry) and experience the church as a place where shared values and customs are reinforced, second-generation Korean Americans attend the EM (English Ministry) and often experience the church as a place where Eastern and Western values are in conflict. As Ken Fong notes,

> Even with a more American mindset, these Asian Americans often find themselves living at the intersection of two different worlds. In the world of larger American society, they know that they can move about more comfortably and garner wider acceptance due to their more westernized upbringing. In a church setting, there are many who would feel more at home in a white congregation than in an Asian one that was dominated by immigrant attitudes. Or they might feel equally uncomfortable in both. But being marginal ethnics, they still have ties to their ethnic roots, ties that they have no desire to sever. In fact, many of the core traditional values of their Asian culture continue to influence their decision. (1990, p. 46; cited in Rah, 2009, p. 183)

Navigating multiple worlds frequently results in frustration and inner conflict. Yet liminal spaces can be productive sites from which to interrogate the nature of our faith. One such area we wish to explore is the biblical virtue of humility. On the one hand, second-generation Korean

Americans learn early on, in church and in the home, that humility is necessary to maintain social order. On the other hand, their encounter with American individualism—the view of the majority culture—raises doubts about virtues that prioritize the collective over the individual. We argue that a biblical, Christ-shaped humility speaks to the cultural tensions that second-generation Korean American Christians navigate.

Western Perspectives on Humility

Although there is no universally accepted definition of humility in Western cultures, having low self-focus and being other-oriented are prominent themes. Dictionaries have typically defined humility as holding oneself in low regard, a trait of meekness, and self-abasement. Meagher et al. (2015), in their article published in the *Journal of Research in Personality*, composed a description of humility noting its multidimensional construct: humility most commonly includes "an accurate or moderate assessment of one's own abilities, being open to new ideas, having a low self-focus, and being able to acknowledge one's own mistakes" (Meagher et al., 2015, p. 36). Clinical Psychologist Elizabeth Krumrei-Mancuso (2017) noted that definitions of humility also include having low self-focus and being other-oriented.

In investigating personality lexicons of diverse languages and cultures, Ashton and Lee (2007) created a six-dimensional structure known as the HEXACO model of personality. The authors identified honesty-humility as a personality trait that

> represents the tendency to be fair and genuine in dealing with others, in the sense of cooperating with others even when one might exploit them without suffering retaliation... high levels of Honesty-Humility are associated with decreased opportunities for personal gains from the exploitation of others but also with decreased risks of losses from withdrawal of cooperation by others. (Ashton and Lee, 2007, p. 156)

Christian psychologists Peter Hill and Elizabeth Laney (2016) present humility as a hypo-egoic phenomenon that involves a nondefensive willingness to see oneself accurately by acknowledging one's personal limitations, combined with an appreciation for the strengths and contributions of other people from which one can learn. They also claim, based on Davis, Worthington, and Hook's (2010; 2011) model of relational humility, that "humility is not a trait that is practiced, or even developed, in isolation. Humility is inherently a relational concept, as its definition proposes an outward focus and some degree of prosocial orientation" (Hill and Laney, 2016, p. 247). They also stated:

> [Humble people] tend to view themselves as being anchored within a larger community, leading to a sense of connectedness to others or to something outside of themselves. This low focus on themselves and corresponding sense of connectedness to something outside of them enables humble persons to transcend self-preoccupation and increase the potential for prosocial concern. (Hill and Laney, 2016, p. 244)

Depending on the scholar, then, Western perspectives on humility emphasize either the disposition of an individual (i.e., an individual trait) or the relation of individual to others (i.e., being other-oriented), or some permutation of the two. We affirm that there is value to each of these perspectives. Yet any account of humility that conceives of this virtue in terms of personal self-abasement, whether freely chosen or societally imposed, overlooks the most critical element of "biblical" humility: not merely the absence of pride or low self-regard, but the cultivation of right relationship with the creator God (cf. Macaskill 2018, 67).

Eastern Perspectives on Humility

East Asian societies have emphasized, and continue to emphasize, the virtue of humility more than most other societies (Herzberg and Herzberg, 2012, p. 24). Humility is seen in individuals, in their relationships with others, and in the very culture and language itself. For instance, after preparing a grand feast for a guest, it is common for the host to declare that there is nothing to eat. People are trained to speak little about their accomplishments lest others become embarrassed or lose face in comparison. Children are taught to be humble and are reprimanded for being braggadocious.

Herzberg and Herzberg (2012) argue that because Asian countries, especially China, were so densely populated, people of these cultures had to emphasize the good of the group over the individual (p. 24). If people did not choose to live in harmony, there would be great conflict due to just the lack of physical space. Hence, the physical environment itself prompted meekness and group coherence.

East Asian values are often identified as being synonymous with Confucian values (Shin and Silzer, 2016, p. 107). School-aged children are required to memorize sayings and proverbs that date back to the teachings of Confucius some 2,500 years ago. And Confucian teachings are responsible for regulating hierarchical structural distinctions and expectations for social behavior.

Confucius attributed the political disorder of his day to the lack of *li*, "propriety" or "proper conduct" (Shin and Silzer, 2016, p. 140). Shin and Silzer note,

> *Li* is not just appropriately performing a social role, but also knowing the appropriate behavior expected of one's role in various social contexts...Confucius proposed that *li* should be learned through the social interactions within five hierarchical relationships (ruler to subject, parent to child, husband to wife, older to younger, and friend to friend). (2016, p. 141)

The individual members of the body politic learn *li* by performing their assigned social roles, which in turn, ensures the social order. If an individual does not perform and internalize *li*, severe cultural and relational consequences may follow. These consequences may include not only being ostracized from the group, but also bringing shame and dishonor to one's family. (There are "113 prototypical terms for shame in the Chinese language, divided into six clusters of meaning" [Lau, 2020, p. 189].) Moreover, there is at least the potential, as Shin and Silzer (2016) note, for "Confucian values [to] contribute to a sense of duty without underlying positive motivation" (p. 150).

Second-generation Korean Americans wrestle with the notion of humility as "a sense of duty without underlying positive motivation." Yet the choice is not as simple as turning from one version of humility (Eastern) to another (Western), for what we encounter in much of Western Christianity, especially in forms of American evangelicalism, is an approach to humility that is radically individualistic. That is, when the virtue of humility is embedded within an evangelical tradition based on "accountable freewill individualism" (Emerson and Smith, 2000, p. 76), or "the gospel of personal sin management" (Edwards, 2020, p. 33), it becomes yet another metric by which Christians measure personal piety. The community remains necessary, to be sure, but only insofar as it provides the means for the individual self to grow: an "I" needs a "you" with which it may exercise and measure "my humility."

This notion of modern individualism, a characteristic of U.S. culture (and especially of white evangelicalism; see Emerson and Smith, 2000, p. 77), involves an entire way of seeing the world. As Grant Macaskill notes,

> When we speak, rather casually, of modern 'individualism,' we often deploy the term as if it simply denotes the pursuit of one's own interests at the expense of a community. In truth, however, the term

points to an entire system of thinking about the individual self as if it were something that has an autonomous identity; the moral dimension of individualism is wrapped up with a deeper issue about how selves are conceived. (2018, p. 81)

Given the unraveling of the moral self in Western culture (see, e.g., MacInytre, 1988), immigrant Christian communities have every reason to resist the allure of "American individualism." (This is of course easier said than done, especially when the churches of the majority culture hold forth "individualism" as the clear and imperative "biblical worldview.")

In fact, the traditional values of East Asian societies share much in common with the biblical authors. For example, Te-Li Lau (2020) has shown that Confucius is much closer to Paul when it comes to the concepts of shame and propriety than most Americans are (pp. 188–203). Asian and Asian American Christians are correct to emphasize that Scripture imagines "communities that foster communitarianism and interdependence" (Lau, 2020, p. 200). The problem with Confucian humility, then, is not that Confucius prioritized the collective, or that *li* (propriety or proper conduct) tends to function as an extrinsic social pressure (both of these dynamics are readily apparent in the "humility" lexicon of the Bible.) The issue, rather, is that Scripture construes humility as Christ-shaped and Spirit-driven. That is, humility flows out of union with Christ by the energizing power of the Holy Spirit.

Christ-Shaped, Spirit-Filled Humility

Scripture is replete with summons to humility and lowliness. Jesus taught his disciples that "the poor in spirit" and "the meek" are heirs of the kingdom of heaven and of the renewed cosmos (Matt 5:3, 5), concepts he no doubt learned from studying the Torah, Prophets, and Psalms. Later in Matthew, he beckons the crowds, "Come to me, all you who are weary and burdened, and I will give you rest. Take my yoke upon you and learn from me, for I am gentle and humble in heart, and you will find rest for your souls. For my yoke is easy and my burden is light" (Matt 11:28–29, NIV). The humble Messiah thus instructs his followers in his way of humility.

The New Testament is clear that the humble way of Jesus is the way of the God of Israel (cf. Mark 1:3). Paul makes this point explicit in the poem he presents to the holy ones in Philippi:

> Who, being in the form of God,
>> did not consider equality with God
>>> something to be used to his

> own advantage;
> rather, he made himself nothing
> by taking the form of a
> slave,
> being born in human likeness.
> And being found in appearance as a
> human,
> he humbled himself
> by becoming obedient unto death—
> even death on a cross!
> Therefore God exalted him to the
> highest place
> and gave him the name that is above
> every name,
> that at the name of Jesus every knee
> should bow,
> in heaven and on earth an under
> the earth,
> and every tongue acknowledge that
> Jesus Christ is Lord,
> to the glory of God the Father. (Phil 2:6–11, NIV slightly adapted)

This poem has received an enormous amount of scholarly attention (see, e.g., Wright, 1986; Hooker, 1990; Oakes, 2001; Eastman, 2010; Fletcher-Louis, 2020). For our purposes, the crucial observation concerns the "mindset" (*phronēsis*) of the Son of God (Phil 2:5). Paul celebrates the Son who refused to exploit his status but, instead, chose to empty himself and to assume adamic humanity. Indeed, the incarnate Son humbled himself in unwavering obedience to the Father—even to the point of death by crucifixion. And precisely because of this, the Father gladly exalted the Son and bestowed upon him the divine name: Lord Jesus Christ! (Phil 2:10–11; cf. Isa 45:23).

As is often the case with encomium (a speech focused on praise), the apostle's interest is not simply to praise the cosmic ruler but also to inculcate his "mindset" in the ethos of the community. That is, Paul wants the Messiah's *phronēsis* to govern his body and its various members: "Let the same mind be in you (*touto phroneite en humin*) that was in Christ Jesus" (Phil 2:5; cf. 2:2). The verb *phroneō* occurs ten times in Philippians and entails the "comprehensive pattern of thinking, feeling, and acting" (Fowl, 2005, p.6) that undergirds the moral reasoning of the community (cf. Johnson, 2003). The Pauline imperative is thus for the body collective to be governed by and to embody a Christ-shaped *phronēsis*, the pattern of divine humility and humiliation disclosed in the encomium.

Such humility undergirds the imperative, "in humility value others above yourselves" (Phil 2:3, NIV). The members of the body are to regard their interests, privileges, and status as Christ regarded his (2:6). In so doing, Paul calls the holy ones in Philippi to the inhabit the new space designated "in Christ" (Thate, 2014). Within this space, humility is not an abstract virtue but participation in the life and life-pattern of the incarnate Son. Paul envisages the telos of life as the imitation of Christ, and he calls on the Philippians to do the same, that is, to become "co-imitators" (3:17).

The apostle implores the Philippians to assume the Christ-shaped *phronēsis* precisely because he is convinced that the Holy Spirit is at work "among you." The inferential imperative of 2:12, "therefore, my dear friends...continue to work out your salvation with fear and trembling," only makes sense in light of the supportive claim of verse 13, "for it is God who works in you to will and to act in order to fulfill his good purposes" (NIV). The apostle's language entails, as Susan Eastman (2017) aptly states,

> a thoroughly intersubjective notion of human personhood, in which God works conatively, cognitively, and effectively within the person, yet the human agent remains distinct and addressable by the imperative, "Work out your salvation." Paul links the divine indicative to the human imperative, and God's action to human action, resulting in the language of "willing" and "working," with its implications of an effective union of thought and action, initiative and follow-through. (Eastman, 2017, p. 128)

Each person learns to internalize humility (or more broadly, *li*) through their participation in the social body (so Confucius). The critical distinction is that Christ-shaped humility is generated by the self-emptying Son of God and actualized in the community by the Holy Spirit.

Conclusion and Implications

Christ-shaped humility speaks to the cultural tensions and social pressures second-generation Korean American Christians currently face. First, it grounds our understanding of humility in the incarnation, which, as Macaskill (2018) notes, is "[t]he crucial element that binds the individual, the communal, and the cosmic together in Paul's narrative" (p. 86). Christ then, is both the generative source and, through the Spirit, is the effective cause of *li* (propriety or proper conduct).

Second, we affirm that biblical humility is a *communal* virtue.

Humility is what the body collective does when it embodies and participates in the Jesus story as outlined by Paul in Philippians 2:6–11. Second-generation Korean Americans can have confidence that many of the values they have inherited, such as a communitarian account of humility, resonate with Scripture's vision for church. The creator God does indeed call us to maintain a particular kind of social order, one governed by the *phronēsis* of the incarnate Son of God.

Second-generation Korean American Christians continue to navigate complex cultural tensions, including, as we have focused on in this article, competing notions of humility. In light of this reality, we offer a few suggestions for churches and pastors.

First, it is essential that churches create structures and spaces for second-generation Korean Americans to explore their Christian identity *while straddling competing cultural tensions*. For example, Korean American churches might evaluate the extent to which they have considered the particular interests and concerns of the second generation. This would involve an assessment of current leadership structures, the content of preaching and teaching, and long-term plans for innovation, among other things. Multiethnic churches, or churches that aspire to be multiethnic, should consider offering cultural competency courses and/or seminars that attend to traditional East Asian values and how East Asian immigrant communities have navigated the dominant US culture.

Second, many pastors and faith leaders recognize that American individualism presents serious challenges to a biblical vision of life together. We would argue that second-generation Korean Americans are well-positioned to guide those who see the world primarily through an individualistic lens to a richer, more communal (i.e., biblical) understanding of their faith (Rah 2009, p. 187).

Lastly, it is vital to the mission and witness of the church that we continue to explore *theologically* how different cultures see the world. For better or for worse (probably a bit of both) American evangelicalism has had an outsized influence on global Christianity. But the Bible is not a "Western" book, nor is Christianity the possession of "Western culture." The goal is not to set East and West in conflict but to live more fully into our identity as God's children: to receive our fellow image-bears as gifts, to learn from one another, and most importantly, to love one another well.

References

Ashton, M. C., & Lee, K. (2007). Empirical, theoretical, and practical advantages of the HEXACO model of personality structure. *Personality and Social*

Psychological Review, 11(2), 150-166.
https://doi.org/10.1177/1088868306294907

Davis, D. E., Hook, J. N., Worthington, E. L., Van Tongeren, D. R., Gartner, A. L., Jennings, D. J., & Emmons, R. A. (2011). Relational humility: Conceptualizing and measuring humility as a personality judgment. *Journal of Personality Assessment, 93*, 225–234.
https://doi.org/10.1080/00223891.2011.558871

Davis, D. E., Worthington, E. L., Jr., & Hook, J. N. (2010): Humility: Review of measurement strategies and conceptualization as personality judgment. *Journal of Positive Psychology, 4*, 243–252.
https://doi.org/10.1080/17439761003791672

Eastman, S. G. (2017). *Paul and the person: Reframing Paul's anthropology.* Eerdmans.

Edwards, D. R. (2020). *Might from the margins: The Gospel's power to turn the tables on injustice.* Herald Press.

Emerson, M. O., and Smith, C. (2000). *Divided by faith: Evangelical religion and the problem of race in America.* Oxford University Press.

Fletcher-Louis, C. (2020). The being that is in a manner equal with God (Phil 2:6c): A self-transforming, incarnational, divine ontology." *Journal of Theological Studies, 71*(2), 581-627.

Fong, K. U. (1990). *Insights for growing Asian-American ministries.* EverGrowing.

Fowl, S. E. (2005). Philippians. *Two horizons New Testament commentary.* Eerdmans.

Herzberg, Q. X. & Herzberg, L. (2012). *Chinese proverbs and popular sayings: With observations on culture and language.* Stone Bridge Press.

Hill, P. and Laney, E. (2016). Beyond self-interest: Humility and the quieted self. In *The Oxford Handbook of Hypo-egoic Phenomena,* edited by K. W. Brown and M. R. Leary.
https://doi.org/10.1093/oxfordhb/9780199328079.013.16

Hofstede, G. & Hofstede, G. (2005). *Cultures and organizations*: *Software of the mind.* McGraw-Hill.

Johnson, L. T. (2003). Transformation of the mind and moral discernment in Paul." Pp. 215–36 in *Early Christianity and classical culture: Comparative studies in honor of Abraham J. Malherbe,* J. T. Fitzgerald, T. H. Olbricht, & L. M. White, Eds. Brill.

Krumrei-Mancuso, E. (2017). Intellectual humility and prosocial values: Direct and mediated effects. *The Journal of Positive Psychology, 12*(1), 13-28.

Lau, T.-L. (2020). *Defending shame: Its formative power in Paul's letters.* Baker Academic.

Macaskill, G. (2018). *The New Testament and intellectual humility.* Oxford University Press.

MacIntyre, A. (1988). *Whose justice? Which rationality?* Notre Dame University Press.

Meagher, B., Leman, J., Bias, J., Latendresse, S., and Rowatt, W. (2015). Contrasting self-report and consensus ratings of intellectual humility and arrogance. *Journal of Research in Personality. 58*, 35-45.

Oakes, P. (2001). *Philippians: From people to letter.* SNTSMS 110. Cambridge University Press.

Oh, J. H. (2004) "The Korean immigrant church in America: Discipleship in the 21st century". (Ph.D. diss., Talbot School of Theology, Biola University).

Park, S. K. (1997) "An analysis of English ministries in the Korean church in Southern California." (Ph.D. diss., Fuller Theological Seminary).

Rah, S.-C. (2009). *The next evangelicalism: Freeing the church from Western cultural captivity.* InterVarsity Press.

Shin, B. & Silzer, S. (2016). *Tapestry of grace: Untangling the cultural complexities in Asian American life and ministry.* Wipf & Stock.

Thate, M. J. (2014). "Paul, *Φρόνησις,* and participation: The shape of space and the reconfiguration of place in Paul's Letter to the Philippians." Pages 281–327 in *"In Christ" in Paul: Explorations in Paul's Theology of Union and Participation.* Edited by Michael J. Thate, Kevin J. Vanhoozer, and Constantine R. Campbell. WUNT 2/384. Mohr Siebeck.

Wright, N. T. (1986). "*Harpagmos* and the meaning of Philippians 2:5–11." *Journal of Theological Studies. 37,* 321–52.

About the Authors

Eunice Hong, PhD (Biola University), is Assistant Professor of Intercultural Studies and Ministry at Cornerstone University in Grand Rapids, Michigan. She recently published a book chapter *Contextualization of the Gospel for North Korean ideology: Engaging with North Korean refugees.* Email: eunice.hong@cornerstone.edu

Max Botner, PhD (University of Saint Andrews), is Associate Professor of Bible and Theology at William Jessup University, Rocklin, California. He is the author *Jesus Christ as the Son of David in the Gospel of Mark* which was awarded the 2021 Manfred Lautenschläger Award for Theological Promise. Email: mbotner@jessup.edu

GREAT COMMISSION
RESEARCH JOURNAL
2022, Vol. 14(2) 31-42

Applying Paul's Areopagus Model to Generation Z

Tanita Maddox
Young Life

Abstract

The members of Generation Z are today's adolescents and young professionals, bringing with them their own culture. This culture requires other generations to use a cross-cultural approach to evangelism, as modeled by Paul in Athens (Acts 17:16-34). Paul observed the Athenian culture, built rapport, used common language with his audience, found common ground as a cultural doorway for his message, and redefined the audience's understanding of the relationship between God and humans. The same steps can be applied to gospel proclamation to Generation Z for effective and relevant evangelism.

Key Words: Generation Z, Gen Z, Paul, Areopagus, evangelism

The topic and the ideas in this article are addressed more extensively in the author's doctoral thesis on file at Phoenix Seminary in Scottsdale, AZ (Maddox, 2020).

Generation Z (Gen Z) has arrived, filling the rooms of middle schools, high schools, colleges, and workplaces, but not churches. Accompanying the arrival of Gen Z are the complexities brought about by social media and smartphones (Twenge, 2017), increased levels of anxiety, depression, and isolation (Twenge, 2018, pp. 93–118), and biblical illiteracy (Copan & Litwak, 2014, p. 36). Gen Z is morally fluid: their moral standards and ideals shift over time and with different circumstances (Barna Group, 2018, p. 55). For Gen Z, what is morally unacceptable in one situation (e.g., cheating) is acceptable in another situation (e.g., cheating is permissible when the test is biased; Jensen et al., 2002). Absolute or universal truth has been replaced with a personal or individualized definition of truth; in other words, truth is determined by each individual (Barna Group, 2018, p. 65). Gen Z brings a culture of its own, one most churches do not understand.

It is critical to recognize that, for older generations (Millennials, Generation X, and Baby Boomers) who minister to Gen Z, this ministry is not only cross-generational, but also cross-cultural. Like any culture, Gen Z brings its own set of values, norms, taboos, mores, language, and dress, distinguishing the culture of Gen Z from others (Livermore, 2009, p. 29). In this way, older generations ministering to Gen Z are cross-cultural ministers. Thus, gospel proclamation to Gen Z requires a different approach to evangelism than those used with previous generations, necessitating cultural intelligence to understand the audience and communicate effectively. Because of this, contextualization principles historically applied to ethnic or geographical cross-cultural evangelism can and should be applied to gospel proclamation to Generation Z.

Cross-cultural contextualization of the gospel for a specific generation, versus culture based on ethnicity, has often been ignored as a topic of study. Paul's Areopagus speech (Acts 17:16-34) is an example of cross-cultural contextualization and evangelism that can be applied to reaching Gen Z. Because Paul's speech provides an example of cross-cultural contextualization, and those ministering cross-culturally to Gen Z require skills in contextualization, studying Paul's Areopagus speech can contribute to the discussion regarding contextualization of the gospel to Gen Z. Paul's Mars Hill method of gospel proclamation can be applied to a Gen Z audience in a way that appeals to their cultural values as a means to share gospel truth.

Western cultural philosophies increasingly reflect the pagan Athenian culture to which Paul was preaching (Copan & Litwak, 2014, p. 37). While Gen Z is not pre-Christian, as the ancient Athenians were, they are post-Christian, with little-to-no cultural reference to matters of the Christian faith and prioritizing their own cultural beliefs over those of the Bible (Barna Group, 2018, p. 36). Moreover, Gen Z is biblically illiterate, just as the Athenians were biblically illiterate.

This article proposes that common Gen Z cultural values can be utilized as doorways to effectively proclaim the gospel to Gen Z, as modeled by Paul in Acts 17:16-34 (see also Maddox, 2020). This article focuses on Gen Z and the cultural values and beliefs of this generation for the purpose of identifying cultural doorways for gospel proclamation and cultivating what is good news for Generation Z. This article proposes Gen Z's values create a sort of cultural doorway, an entrance point, through which gospel proclamation can be received in an understandable and relevant way. The aim of the evangelist is to engage with culture in order to transform it (Flemming, 2005, p. 265). If churches understand the values and worldview of Gen Z, they can respond with relevant proclamation and discipleship that allows this new generation to engage its values in a way that reflects the Kingdom of God.

Paul's Cross-Cultural Proclamation at Mars Hill

Paul's message at the Areopagus in Acts 17:16-34 is often applied within missiology, cross-cultural ministry, and gospel proclamation. Paul's Areopagus speech provides a skillfully crafted, culturally sensitive, and sophisticated model for evangelism, "enabling his audience right away to feel at home" (Flemming, 2005, p. 74). Paul's approach in Athens includes observing his audience's culture (Acts 17:16, 23), building rapport (Acts 17:22), finding common ground to effectively share his message (Acts 17:23-24), using culturally appropriate language (Acts 17:28), and redefining the relationship between humanity and God (Acts 17:24-31).

Paul lived in and understood three different cultural contexts: Second-Temple Judaism, the Roman Empire, and Hellenistic culture (Wright, 2009, pp. 3–5). This is not unlike the experience of a Christian in the United States today, who is a member of the following cultural contexts, among others: the Christian Church, one's own generation, and the post-Christian, capitalist Western world. In some ways, the evangelist to Gen Z must become culturally trilingual, as Paul was, to share the gospel message. Paul demonstrated in Acts 17:16-34, that proclaimers of the gospel can approach people within their social and cultural world and also guide those people and their values toward the gospel (Schnabel, 2012, p. 176).

Gen Z as a Culture

This article argues Gen Z should be treated as its own culture with its own cultural context. Generations have their own culture and unique sets of "mental software" (Hofstede et al., 2010, pp. 5, 18.). David Livermore notes the cultural differences between generations "can equal" those between socioethnic groups (Livermore, 2009, p. 29). Gen Z possesses its own distinct attitudes, beliefs, social norms, and behaviors, defining it as its own culture (Seemiller & Grace, 2016, p. 1). While Gen Z could be considered a subculture or microculture within a greater culture, it can be deduced from their own distinct values, beliefs, language, and systems that Gen Z possesses its own cultural identity (Howell, 2016, p. 66). Born between 1999-2013, the bulk of Generation Z are adolescents, and it can be difficult to separate and identify specifically what is generational and what is a developmental stage within this generation. However, when it comes to evangelism and contextualization of the gospel to Gen Z, at least at this point in time, both are important and are in fact, intertwined in understanding Gen Z. This article discusses treating Gen Z as a culture of its own in order to help previous generations engage in cross-cultural evangelism as the preferred method of gospel proclamation.

Paul's Five Principles Applied to Generation Z

Paul employed five principles in his Areopagus speech: 1) he observed the culture, 2) he built rapport with his audience, 3) he used common language, 4) he utilized a cultural doorway as a gateway for proclamation, and 5) he redefined the relationship between humanity and the divine. These principles are commonly discussed in missiology and cross-cultural evangelism. This article will now apply Paul's five principles from Acts 17:16-34 to the work of gospel proclamation to Gen Z.

Observe Gen Z Culture

The first principle outlined in Acts 17:16-34 was to become familiar with the audience's culture. Paul is a student, "a careful observer," of the culture around him (Sampley, 2016, p. 392). Paul "walked around and looked carefully at [the Athenians'] objects of worship," even reading the inscriptions (Acts 17:23). Understanding the Athenians' culture, Paul used their language to communicate to his audience in their terms (Copan & Litwak, 2014, p. 14). He "intentionally uses the philosophical language of his audience" to translate the Christian message for a pagan audience (Flemming, 2005, p. 79). He knew pagan poetry familiar to his audience and cited some of those poets in Acts 17:28. Paul's observation of the Athenian culture allowed him to identify familiar poetry and rhetoric for his audience.

Churches can see Gen Z's values of authenticity, safety, inclusion, personal freedom, and the belief of inherent dignity of all human beings. While these values may have timeless aspects, the context and translation of these values, and how Gen Z both experiences and expresses them, are distinct to their generational identity. The value of authenticity is of utmost importance to Gen Z and has been formed, in part, by social media. Generation Z had early access to interactive technology and is "tech-fluent."(J. Walter Thompson Intelligence, 2012, p. 3). Because they are aware social media is full of falsities and façades, Gen Z attributes trustworthiness and credibility to transparency (Witt & Baird, 2018, p. 46) and is highly attuned to the fact that a person may have multiple identities or versions of oneself, even if these have conflicting values or morals. Gen Z wants to know who is actually who they say they are or who they present themselves as. Because they are immersed in the false realities of social media and the internet, Gen Z's principle rule is to look for those who can be themselves (Twenge, 2018, pp. 106–107, 286). This thirst for authenticity extends to the need for authentic relationships and real-life connections with people rather than digital ones (Seemiller & Grace, 2016, pp. 62, 94).

Gen Z defines authenticity based on its own terms. For example, generally, Gen Z views Christians as intolerant (Twenge, 2018, p. 139), hypocritical (Barna Group, 2018, p. 29), and judgmental (Barna Group, 2018, p. 30), among other descriptors. If a Christian does not admit to being guilty of such things, a member of Gen Z is likely to describe that Christian as inauthentic. For example, a Christian may share about his or her failures, shortcomings, and even areas of embarrassment or shame, but if these do not directly relate to the areas where Gen Z believes Christians are hiding or being dishonest, then that Christian is still likely to be described as inauthentic by Gen Z. When it comes to evangelism, Gen Z is looking for an authentic source, as well as an authentic message, rooted in transparency, honesty, and credibility as they view the world.

Gen Z is coming of age during a global pandemic, the proliferation of social media, and a continued trend of school shootings. Gen Z wants to feel safe all of the time, which includes physical, emotional, psychological, and perceived safety (Twenge, *iGen*, p. 159). This has led to the following belief: If something is not absolutely safe, it is dangerous and must be avoided (Lukianoff & Haidt, 2018, p. 177).

Gen Z values belonging, an expression of acceptance and inclusivity, (Brown, 2014, p. 11), and believes themselves to be more open-minded than previous generations (Premack, 2018). Their cultural context reflects increasing acceptance of people or ideas that may have been traditionally rejected or restricted by older or past generations. Gen Z has only existed in a world with a black president, legalized gay marriage, legalized marijuana in many states, and females in high-ranking political offices (Weise, 2019, pg. 24). Seventy percent of Gen Z teenagers think it is "definitely or probably acceptable to be born one gender but identify as another" (Williams et al., 2019, p. 274). Because Gen Z views Christians as intolerant, as mentioned earlier, it can be deduced they have not witnessed churches embracing all those whom Gen Z accepts.

There is a clear link between perceived or actual rejection by others and experienced depression (Williams et al., 2019, p. 274). This impact of acceptance, or lack thereof, on Gen Z's well-being reflects how deeply rooted the value of acceptance is. Gen Z's cultural understanding of freedom is related to the generation's cultural value of acceptance. To live authentically for Gen Z, one should be able to do or be whatever one wants. For Gen Z, personal freedom should not be limited or restricted because restriction prevents a person from living authentically. Thus, obstructing personal freedom is obstructing authenticity, which ultimately communicates rejection, not acceptance, of one's "true," authentic self. Relativism not only protects personal freedom but allows for the acceptance and inclusion of others (Barna Group, 2018, p. 69). Gen Z subscribes to the cultural fear of exclusion or rejection: They are worried that belief in universal truth could lead to "oppressing those who disagree" (Copan & Litwak, 2014, p. 50). The values of tolerance and acceptance became more important than believing in universal truth, creating a system in which Gen Z Christians deny their own beliefs if said beliefs are perceived as intolerant (Nappa, 2012, p. 73). Gen Z would rather be fully accepting of others than commit to a truth that rejects any belief system or person. Because Gen Z believes faith restricts personal freedom, many Gen Zers avoid it (Kageler & Clark, 2014, p. 56).

While the need for personal freedom is important to Gen Z, this generation also values social justice and fighting for the dignity of all people, especially the outcasts or oppressed; they long for justice (Gould, 2019, p. 31). They strive to be socially aware and make the world a better place yet they have a complex relationship with acceptance and social justice (Shankar, 2019, p. 15). After all, the very concept of justice hinges upon defining what is wrong, what needs to be rectified, and identifying the values or actions that need to be rejected. Understanding this tension can help the evangelist decipher what is good news to a generation that longs for both acceptance and justice.

Build Rapport

Paul also exercised the use of a *captatio benevolentiae, words of praise,* in the opening of his speech with his Athenian audience to gain rapport (Rothschild, 2014, pp. 52–53). In Acts 17:22, Paul built rapport by connecting with his audience's values, calling Athenians δεισιδαιμονεστέρους (*deisidaimonesteros*), which translates as devout (Grimm et al., 1963, p. 127). Paul also acknowledged the Athenian's respect for the divine (Holladay, 1988, p. 1102). Many scholars agree it is likely Paul was speaking positively. This also fits within the rhetorical fashion, which is why δεισιδαιμονεστέρους should be translated in a positive way rather than as negative or rebuking. If this was Paul's first line in addressing the council at Areopagus, it was likely in order to communicate respect and honor to his audience.

The first sentence in a proclamation to a Gen Z audience can be powerful when it identifies, addresses, and honors a Gen Z cultural value. An anecdotal reflection on how Gen Z is described in the media and by older generations will often result in words like weak, fragile, snowflake, entitled, over-emotional, or over-sensitive. Building rapport with a Gen Z audience means changing the message communicated by older generations. For example, rather than refer to Gen Z as anxious and weak, one can acknowledge the courage and strength it takes to navigate the world of social media and/or "cancel culture." It could be stated as the following, "Gen Z! I can see in every way you are courageous and strong, navigating the constant toxic messages coming to you from social media. I cannot imagine what it is like to grow up in a time where simply asking the 'wrong' question can lead to public shaming and rebuking of your 'ignorance.' I am in awe of your continued strength and bravery." This positive messaging acknowledges the positive attributes of the generation and builds rapport.

Find Common Ground

Paul established common ground with his audience and used a cultural doorway for his message. In Acts 17:23, Paul highlights a "point of agreement" with the Epicurean audience by saying he will preach about the "unknown god" (Schnabel, 2012, p. 730). Paul chose to build a bridge to his audience's culture and worldview, rather than yell "across a yawning cultural gap" (Wright, 1997, p. 80). Then, Paul turned from the common ground to teach about the one true God of the Bible (Schnabel, 2012, p. 732). Paul presented a new idea of the divine, arguing that "we should not think that the divine being is like gold or silver or stone—an image made by human design and skill" (Acts 17:29).

In the same way, Gen Z values can provide common ground for the gospel message. The Gen Z value of acceptance is reflected in a call to respond to the gospel. Gen Zers can trust in a God who will accept them: "Whoever comes to me I will never drive away" (John 6:37). The rejection that Gen Z fears in life can be alleviated when they are assured that they can "approach God's throne of grace with confidence" (Hebrews 4:16).

Gen Z's values of social justice and the dignity of human life can also provide common ground. After all, human dignity is rooted in how God treats humans with dignity as bearers of his image (Vorster, 2007, pp. 334, 337). Murder is taken seriously because it is taking the life of someone made in the Image of God (Genesis 9:6). This common ground reinforces the divine underpinning of human life. Discussion around the image of God and the dignity of all human life allows Gen Z to engage their generational values through a biblical lens provided by the evangelist.

Use Common Language

In his speech to the Athenians, Paul demonstrates the use of a common language as he "intentionally uses the philosophical language of his audience" (Flemming, 2005, p. 79). He addressed the Epicurean and Stoic philosophies in his speech (Copan & Litwak, 2014, p. 72). As stated earlier, Paul quotes his audience's poets in the middle of his speech (Act 17:28). Using common language contributes to contextualization in gospel proclamation.

Using language in common with Gen Z does not necessarily mean using Gen Z vernacular or slang. It could mean quoting a song, artist, or influencer familiar to the Gen Z audience. More practically, using common language means utilizing terminology that lines up with their espoused values in a way that is familiar to them. For example, words like acceptance and authentic may perk their ears, but they will be paying particular attention to the context in which those terms are used. More specifically, a church, pastor, or evangelist from older generations may feel they are being authentic, genuine, and transparent; however, as touched upon earlier, if that authenticity or transparency is not executed in the way Gen Z is expecting, those attempts at genuine connection will only create an impression of inauthenticity. In a proclamation setting, an evangelist can admit to his/her need for Jesus by humbly admitting to such things as being judgmental or hypocritical (descriptions of Christians employed by Gen Z) while expressing the desire to be authentic to the Gen Z audience. This provides a values-driven, common language.

Redefine the Relationship Between God and Humans

Paul uses common ground and common language, but he does not allow the Athenians to maintain a flawed view of God. Paul departs from the

Stoic belief in divine providence to teaching about "the one true God of biblical revelation" (Schnabel, 2012, p. 732). In Acts 17:24-25, Paul argues idol worship is flawed, further redefining the worship relationship between humans and the divine (Gempf, 1993, p. 52). Paul distinguishes between the created and the Creator, clarifying that it is God who is to be worshiped without being compromised in physical representation (Rost, n.d., p. 123). In his contextualization, Paul moves his audience toward biblical truth.

Contextualization of the gospel for Gen Z allows the gospel to be placed in the language of a cultural moment (Newbigin, 1986, p. 2). By understanding Gen Z and principles of biblical contextualization, older generations ministering to Gen Z can "transmit the gospel...to a radically different" culture than their own (Newbigin, 1986, p. 1). This can include redefining what it means to be free or safe, thus engaging Gen Z's values of freedom and safety without promoting a flawed worldview. If Gen Z views freedom as freedom from any constraint or limitation, the gospel proclamation can include deconstructing that idea of freedom and redefining it in a more biblical sense. The Parable of the Lost Son portrays a son who pursues what he thinks is freedom, only to find himself with nothing (Luke 15:11-32). In fact, his flawed idea of freedom only leads to the opposite. Thus, the gospel proclamation illustrates the nature of true freedom: Freedom comes from Jesus (John 8:36), and in Jesus one will no longer experience slavery (Galatians 5:1). A Gen Z audience, valuing and desiring freedom, can then be encouraged to link this cultural value with a gospel proclamation relevant to their worldview. The gospel proclaimer thereby moves the audience toward a biblical model of freedom rather than a flawed understanding of freedom.

Conclusion

Ministry to Gen Z by older generations is not only cross-generational, but cross-cultural. Gospel proclamation to Gen Z requires a cross-cultural approach to evangelism in order to be effective. Thus, examining and applying Paul's cross-cultural contextualization model employed in Athens provides an effective approach for evangelizing Gen Z (Acts 17:16-34). Paul's method includes: 1) observing the culture, 2) building rapport, 3) using common language, 4) finding a cultural doorway, and 5) redefining the relationship between God and humans.

Because Gen Z has much in common with Paul's Athenian audience, his evangelism methodology can be applied to this generation. This article has demonstrated how common Gen Z cultural values can be utilized as doorways to effectively proclaim the gospel, as modeled by Paul in Acts

17:16-34. Gen Z values of freedom and authenticity can be used as a doorway to share the gospel in a relevant and understandable way, highlighting the good news to Gen Z. If ministers of the gospel understand the values and worldview of Gen Z, they can cultivate a relevant, cohesive message that allows this new generation to engage its values in a way that brings the Kingdom of Heaven down to earth.

References

Barna Group. (2018). *Gen Z: The culture, beliefs and motivations shaping the next generation*. Barna Group.

Brown, M. G. (2014). The impact of adolescent experiences on emerging adult church-based retention. *The Journal of Youth Ministry, 13(1)*, 5–16.

Copan, P., & Litwak, K. D. (2014). *The gospel in the marketplace of ideas: Paul's Mars Hill experience for our pluralistic world*. InterVarsity Press.

Flemming, D. E. (2005). *Contextualization in the New Testament: Patterns for theology and mission*. InterVarsity Press.

Gempf, C. (1993). *Paul at Athens*. In G. F. Hawthorne, R. P. Martin, & D. G. Reid (Eds.), *Dictionary of Paul and his letters* (pp. 51–54). InterVarsity Press.

Gould, P. M. (2019). *Cultural apologetics: Renewing the Christian voice, conscience, and imagination in a disenchanted world*. Zondervan.

Grimm, C., Wilibald, L., Thayer, H., & Wilke, C. G. (1963). *Greek-English lexicon of the New Testament: Being Grimm's Wilke's Clavis Novi Testamenti*. Zondervan.

Hofstede, G., Hofstede, G. J., & Minkov, M. (2010). *Cultures and organizations: Software for the mind*. McGraw-Hill.

Holladay, C. R. (1988). Acts. In the *Harper's Bible Commentary* (pp. 1102–1103). Harper and Row.

Howell, B. (2016). Technology and adoptive youth ministry. In C. Clark (Ed.), *Adoptive youth ministry: Integrating emerging generations into the family*. Baker Academic.

J. Walter Thompson Intelligence. (2012, April). *Gen Z: Digital in Their DNA* (April 2012) [Business]. https://www.slideshare.net/jwtintelligence/f-external-genz041812-12653599/3-INTRODUCTIONGen_Z_is_the_fledgling

Jensen, L., Arnett, J., Feldman, S., & Cauffman, E. (2002). It's wrong, but everybody does it: Academic dishonesty among high school and college students. *Contemporary Educational Psychology*, 27, 209–228. https://doi.org/10.1006/ceps.2001.1088

Kageler, L., & Clark, C. (2014). *Youth ministry in a multifaith society: Forming Christian identity among skeptics, syncretists and sincere believers of other faiths*. InterVarsity Press.

Livermore, D. A. (2009). *Cultural intelligence: Improving Your CQ to engage our multicultural world youth, family, and culture*. Baker Academic.

Lukianoff, G., & Haidt, J. (2018). *The coddling of the American mind: How good intentions and bad ideas are setting up a generation for failure.* Penguin Press.

Maddox, T. (2020). *Gen Z as the Areopagus: Gospel contextualization for a generation.* D.Min. thesis, Phoenix Seminary.

Nappa, M. (2012). *The Jesus survey: What Christian teens really believe and why.* Baker Books.

Newbigin, L. (1986). *Foolishness to the Greeks: The gospel and western culture.* Wm. B. Eerdmans.

Premack, R. (2018, June 20). *Gen Zs never watch TV, are stressed about Snapchat, and are concerned that technology has ruined their mental health—Here's what it's really like to be a teen in 2018.* Business Insider Australia. https://www.businessinsider.com.au/teens-gen-z-generation-z-what-teens-are-like-2018-6

Rost, S. (n.d.). Paul's Areopagus speech in Acts 17: A Paradigm for applying apologetics and missions to non-christian religious movements. In *Encountering new religious movements: A holistic evangelical approach* (pp. 113–136). Kregel Publications.

Rothschild, C. K. (2014). *Paul in Athens: The popular religious context of Acts 17.* Mohr Siebeck.

Sampley, J. P. (2016). Living in an evil aeon: Paul's ambiguous relation to culture (Toward a taxonomy). In *Paul in the Greco-Roman world: A handbook* (Vol. 2, pp. 391–342). Bloomsbury.

Schnabel, E. J. (2012). *Acts.* Zondervan.

Seemiller, C., & Grace, M. (2016). *Generation Z goes to college.* John Wiley & Sons.

Shankar, S. (2019). *Beeline: What spelling bees reveal about Generation Z's new path to success.* Basic Books.

Twenge, J. M. (2017, September). *Have smartphones destroyed a generation?* https://www.theatlantic.com/magazine/archive/2017/09/has-the-smartphone-destroyed-a-generation/534198/

Twenge, J. M. (2018). *iGen: Why today's super-connected kids are growing up less rebellious, more tolerant, less happy--and completely unprepared for adulthood (and what this means for the rest of us).* Simon and Schuster.

Vorster, N. (2007). A theological evaluation of the South African constitutional value of human dignity. *Journal of Reformed Theology*, 1(3), 320–339. https://doi.org/10.1163/156973107X251003

Weise, S. (2019). *Instabrain : The new rules for marketing to Generation Z.* Sarah Weise.

Williams, A., Giano, Z., & Merten, M. (2019). Running away during adolescence and future homelessness: The amplifying role of mental health. *American Journal of Orthopsychiatry*, 89(2), 268–278. https://doi.org/10.1037/ort0000397

Witt, G. L., & Baird, D. E. (2018). *The Gen Z frequency.* Kogan Page Limited.

Wright, N. T. (1997). *What Saint Paul really said: Was Paul of Tarsus the real founder of Christianity?* William B. Eerdmans Publishing Company.

Wright, N. T. (2009). *Paul: In fresh perspective*. Fortress Press.

About the Author

Tanita Maddox serves as an Associate Regional Director for Young Life. She completed a Masters of Christian Leadership from Fuller Theological Seminary and Doctorate of Ministry from Phoenix Seminary.

SPECIAL SECTION

Introduction to Research on Evangelism

The *Great Commission Research Journal* is honored to present the four papers which have won the 2022 Knox Fellowship Award for Research on Evangelism. Among many good papers submitted, these four stood out for their innovation, their research, and their theology. May the Lord use these for his glory as we work to better equip those around us for the Great Commission.

Research on evangelism is not easy. Some research on evangelism is primarily theoretical and theological, and some research is empirical, conducted by gathering data and analyzing it. The ethical and logistic issues when doing empirical research on evangelism are significant. These four articles represent some of the best of contemporary thought on the subject.

Ken Nehrbass
California Baptist University

Rochelle Scheuermann
Wheaton College

Mark Teasdale
Garrett-Evangelical Theological
Seminary

Yakubu Jakada
Tri-State Bible College

GREAT COMMISSION
RESEARCH JOURNAL
2022, Vol. 14(2) 45-64

Not Just the Sinner's Prayer: People's Experiences with "Stranger-Evangelism"

Kenneth Nehrbass
California Baptist University

Abstract

While churches and Christian concerts are typical loci for evangelism, some Christians also broach the subject of faith with strangers they encounter at their health club, at the beach, or while visiting door-to-door. This study draws from 34 stories of "stranger-evangelism" offered by 11 ministers and laypeople who participated in semi-structured interviews. The central finding of this study is that stranger-evangelism contains a rich variety of experiences that are typical of any ministry: sometimes planned (by proclaiming, inviting, programming, befriending, and serving), and sometimes spontaneously. Participants described the fruit of their efforts along a continuum from rejection to interest, and even to conversion. This article discusses the findings in light of scholarship on breaching social norms and addressing power differentials.

Keywords: evangelism, stranger, ethics, qualitative research, norm expectancy.

Introduction

In 1988, a Vietnam veteran named Bob Wieland spoke to a crowded church in Southern California from his wheelchair. He recounted how he lost his legs after stepping on a mortar round. During his road to recovery, he gained the strength to bench press over 300 pounds, and also found Jesus Christ. He gained notoriety as he completed a three-and-a-half year "Walk for Hunger" (on his hands) across the USA (Skidmore, 1986). Weiland's talk that evening in church ended with a plea for the crowd – many who were strangers to him – to follow Christ. "The journey with Christ begins with your first step. All who would take that step now, stand up and come down the aisle." I walked toward the altar, not too sure what it would mean.

Since then, I have engaged in my own efforts to share Christ with strangers: sometimes through preaching (as Weiland did), sometimes with complete strangers (as part of Cru while in college), and more recently as a missionary in the South Pacific. Even after more than 25 years in the ministry, I am still petrified to approach a stranger to talk about Jesus Christ. I became curious about how laypeople, missionaries, and pastors are able to engage in this special type of ministry. Therefore, I designed this research study to understand people's experiences with stranger-evangelism.

Literature on Stranger-Evangelism

Numerous biblical scholars have exposited the mandate to be involved in evangelism (Saxton, 2017, pp. 73-85). Theologians have noted that evangelism is important for the sake of the Christian's personal growth (Beougher, 2005, p. 121), for the health of the church (Grudem, 1994, p. 868), and, of course, for those who are in danger of hell (Coleman, 1993, p. 94, cf. Saxton 2017).

Much of the literature on evangelism has focused on what Simpson (2003) called "permission evangelism." This includes the "lifestyle evangelism" approach that received much attention during the 1980s (Aldrich, 1983; Moody, 1983). Lifestyle evangelism involves befriending people to the point where the Christian earns an opportunity to share his or her faith journey. Permission evangelism also includes what Johnston (2007) described as "preaching evangelism," where the gospel is presented to people who have elected to come to church.

Another form of permission evangelism is "stadium evangelism" in which the evangelist has implicit permission to share the gospel because people have responded to an invitation (often by their Christian friends) to attend the event. Three empirical studies have been done on "stadium evangelism." First, Whitam (1966) used a decision-making framework to understand teens' responses to messages at evangelistic crusades. Schmidt (1990) collected data after a Luis Palau event, and while the sample size was small ($N = 60$), the statistics gathered were fascinating: Megachurches had a greater advantage over smaller churches in assimilating newcomers who attended the stadium event; the number of baptisms within six months was small, (but still impressive) at 1.5%. Participants said the main strength of the event was mobilizing volunteers in their church; the main weakness was (not surprisingly) follow-up with those who made professions of faith. In the third study, Abrahamse (2021) used linguistic analysis to demonstrate that Dutch media has shifted from skepticism to a more favorable view of Billy Graham's stadium events.

Far less research has been done on "stranger-evangelism"—where the herald often transgresses a social boundary to start a religious conversation with a stranger. Of twelve dissertations related to Cru, none describes the experiences of people who are engaged in this sort of evangelism—not from the perspective of the evangelist nor from that of the "evangelee." Additionally, very little research has been done on people's experiences with planned stranger-evangelism (e.g., door-to-door or beach campaigns) or spontaneous stranger-evangelism (e.g., on an airplane or in the fitness center).

Delineating Stranger-Evangelism

The approach I have termed stranger-evangelism often involves what Cru founder Bill Bright called "aggressive evangelism" (Ingram, 1989, p. 17). Evangelism is "aggressive" when the herald quickly moves to a gospel presentation, even before the evangelee may show interest in the topic. Acts 5:42 describes how the apostles regularly engaged in this highly persuasion-focused approach: "Day after day, in the temple courts and from house to house, they never stopped teaching and proclaiming the good news that Jesus is the Messiah" (NIV).

Stranger-evangelism also involves what Smith (2011), the developer of the "Training for Trainers" model, referred to as "indiscriminate sowing." By this, Smith means we should share the gospel "with everybody, because you never know whom God will choose" (p. 96) to be saved.

Not all evangelism is aggressive or indiscriminate. Yet aggressive stranger-evangelism may be the archetype of the term "evangelism" for many Christians. Johnston's (2007) comprehensive taxonomy of Christian terms explains that some people narrowly use the term "evangelism" to *always* mean sharing the gospel with strangers, and believe it *always* includes an appeal for repentance (pp. 38-39). Johnston avers that the church is not in agreement on whether all Christians should be engaged in this form of proclamation, or whether it is a task set aside for those who expressly have the gift of evangelism.

This brief review of the literature forms the background for my study. How do Christians who engage in stranger-evangelism overcome the social awkwardness? When they do have a moment of the stranger's time, how do they use that time? What is the mark of success or failure for such encounters? Below I describe my methods for researching this study. Then I describe the findings and discuss the results in light of the literature on the social and spiritual aspects of stranger-evangelism.

Methods

The purpose of this descriptive qualitative study was to understand people's experiences with stranger-evangelism. I used purposive sampling to recruit participants who indicated they had experience doing evangelism with strangers. I interviewed 11 people about their regular habits of evangelism which elicited 34 concrete examples of times that they had shared the gospel with a stranger. Table 1 gives more information on the participants.

Table 1: *Participants*

Pseudonym	Occupation
Andrea	Bible translator
Pastor Barry	Pastor of a suburban Southern California church
Pastor Jake	Director of a Christian non-profit, missionary, pastor
Janice	Missionary focusing on evangelism
JB	Author, ministry leader, pastor, evangelist
Kathi	Homemaker
Mary	Healthcare professional
Mike	Entrepreneur
Pastor Ronnie	Pastor of a Mid-Western church
Pastor Steve	Carpenter, pastoral staff at an urban Southern California church
Ted	Missionary mobilizer

I am admittedly an "insider" when it comes to the subject of this research, and I shared a bit of my insider bias at the beginning of this article (namely, that I am simultaneously supportive of and fearful of stranger-evangelism). Methodologists have suggested that insider researchers can mitigate their own biases by having prolonged interviews with multiple participants (Berger, 2013). Therefore, I conducted open-ended, semi-structured interviews to hear participants' own experiences with stranger-evangelism. I transcribed and coded the data in Dedoose software – first at the thought-by-thought level to generate "initial codes," and then at the thematic level (Saldaña, 2015). These thematic codes helped form the answer to the research question. Finally, I carried out "member checks" (Birt, et al., 2016) by sharing the themes with five participants to ensure that my interpretation of the data was aligned with their actual experiences of stranger-evangelism

Findings

The central finding of this study is that stranger-evangelism contains a rich variety of experiences that are typical of any ministry: sometimes planned (by proclaiming, inviting, programming, befriending, and serving), and sometimes spontaneously. Each of these terms will be discussed below. The fruit of such interactions is as variegated as the fruits of any Christian ministry, ranging from rejection to interest, and even to conversion.

I will describe the variety of this richness of this ministry effort below. But first I must revisit the terms "stranger" and "evangelism" in light of participant data.

Defining the Stranger

In many cases, the stranger is not only someone who is unknown, but who is socio-culturally different than the evangelist. Mike (who serves food to the homeless every week) told me, "The people in my neighborhood with jobs and homes don't want to hear about the gospel." In contrast, the homeless are willing to talk about it "because they've all been broken."

Janice explained that "it pays to look like an East Asian sometimes" at her college campus because some students from the Middle East are "so interested in K-Pop or anything Korean or Japanese" that they will strike up a conversation. And a missionary in Southeast Asia leverages her own "difference" to befriend strangers and start religious conversations on the campus. "I ask people about their hijab or bindi dots. I explain that I have not met many Muslims or Hindus." She noted that a Christian in her host country found that leveraging "difference" may work for missionaries, but not for national Christians:

> She told me, "That's easier for you, because you're a foreigner, and genuinely don't know these things. People know that we [nationals] already know what the hijab is or what the bindi dot is, so it's harder for us to start conversations."

Not all stranger-evangelism involves socio-cultural difference. Participants described sharing the gospel at health clubs, restaurants, and in their own neighborhoods, regardless of any differences. The commonality is that all participants had approached people who were unknown to them. "It's hardest to evangelize your own family," Mary told me.

Note that for participants, "stranger" is ideally a temporary status. A missionary challenged me about the use of the term, "At what point does the stranger become a friend?" This desire to move someone from "stranger" to "friend" was shared by multiple participants (as I show throughout the findings section). Whether participants engage in scheduled or spontaneous encounters – and regardless of whether they are befriending, proclaiming, inviting, outreaching, or serving – their hope is that the first interaction will result in a deeper relationship that would result in conversion and discipleship.

Defining Evangelism

As the central finding of this study indicates, evangelism is a fairly fluid term for participants. The actions they described as "stranger-evangelism" involve praying for others and meeting their needs, as well as explaining the core tenets of the Christian faith. (The richness of these actions will be developed throughout the findings section). I was surprised, though, that only three participants in this study explicitly explained to me the kerygma of the gospel as they described "evangelism." For all of these three, the gospel involves confessing a belief in the substitutionary atonement and repenting from sins, with the result of being born again (see John 3:1-21).

Additionally, some people are fluent in multiple types of stranger-evangelism: Pastor Barry and Pastor Ronnie both participate in door-to-door efforts as well as spontaneous evangelistic encounters at the gym. Mike and Kathi pray for people, hand out food, and lead Bible studies in the park.

Motivations for Stranger-Evangelism

Nine of the eleven participants expressly described the awkwardness of approaching strangers to talk about faith. Pastor Jake recognized his efforts on the beach interrupt people's plans; Pastor Barry empathized with those who are less than pleased to have someone come to the door on a Saturday morning. What motivates people to overcome the awkwardness, in an attempt to reach strangers?

Pastor Barry talked to me about motivation:

We have one big, imposing guy on the team. He says, "I know nobody wants to see me on their doorstep. But Jesus saved me. Someone told me about Jesus. And now I've told everyone in my circle. I need to get to a fresh pond."

Ted has a similar sense of paying it forward. He recalls a friend in college who shared the gospel with him. "I'd love to do that for someone else...to go out of my comfort zone to do that...It seems like the Holy Spirit could do a lot."

Mike, an entrepreneur in Florida, was motivated by a supernatural calling. "I was out on a walk praying for my neighborhood. I prayed, 'Lord, send workers.' And God said, 'What about you?' So I started giving out food and sharing the gospel."

Steve described his motivation: "People are separated from God...so I try to shrink that gap...so they can see God is desirable. He's after them." Similarly, Pastor Jake is motivated to warn people about the peril of eternal punishment. He explained:

People around us that we interact with every day are going to hell without the gospel. If I knew they were walking into a building that was on fire, I would do everything I could to stop them from going in.

Jake then invited me to join him on Tuesdays, to overcome my own trepidation of stranger-evangelism.

The Planned Context

As I indicated above, participants' encounters are sometimes planned, and sometimes spontaneous. They described five different types of planned stranger-evangelism: proclaiming, inviting, programming, befriending, and serving. I will discuss each below.

Planned Proclamation

Some participants go to specific venues on a schedule to expressly preach a message about salvation. They have developed strategies for reducing awkwardness and for broaching the topic of faith.

Ted described what may be the quintessential example of planned proclamation: He spent a summer doing "open-air evangelism." His team performed skits in a park to gather a crowd. Then a speaker would share the gospel. Ted did not see much fruit. "People would laugh and smile; but there were very few conversations."

Pastor Jake takes a team each Tuesday night to the pier to explain the path of salvation. He approaches strangers with the prop of a "curved illusion" from Living Waters Ministry:

> Then I say something like, "Hey, I have a question for you guys: Which one of these items looks bigger?" It breaks the tension of "I'm a complete stranger and I'm talking to you." Then I say, "Hey, do you guys go to church?" That starts the conversation. It turns to sharing the gospel from there.

Jake also hands out Starbucks cards in order to start conversations. "I don't give a gospel tract and that's it. I want to engage people. I say, "There's a gospel message in there. Do you go to church?" If he gets a hearing, Jake spends a great deal of time on the concept of sin, and he explains judicial atonement. "It's about getting to the conscience and letting the Holy Spirit...it's not about apologetics." He recounted,

> You can see the moment when the Spirit convicts them.... The goal isn't the sinner's prayer. That's not in Scripture. The goal is repentance. Someone says, "I'm a sinner and I need repentance." So, I walk them through what it means to be sorrowful, to do a U-turn.

Jake is confident that handing out tracts can be efficacious even if people show no initial interest. "I've heard about people who get a gospel tract, throw it in a drawer, and read it six months later, and that's when it hits them."

JB, a prominent church leader in a World class city, spent over twenty years sending out 25 to 50 people each weekend in teams. He modeled his ministry after the evangelist Arthur Blessitt, encouraging the teams to ask people about their eternal destiny:

> It wasn't hard to give a tract; but if they would slow down, we would say, "Can I ask you a question? If you died tonight, do you know that God would let you into heaven?" One out of ten would stop, and one out of ten who stopped would listen.

Planned Invitations

Ten of the eleven participants use invitations as a way of beginning a conversation and then move on to proclamation if the evangelee shows interest. This approach includes inviting people to attend an event or inviting them to pray.

Inviting is less threatening than proclaiming, making the planned invitational approach more accessible to budding evangelists. To those who are too timid to talk, Barry says, "Stand at a respectful distance and just pray." The evangelism teams also have room for those who are too timid for going door-to-door at all:

> If knocking on a stranger's door is just way too much, we have them set up at a park or on a trail, and smile at people. And if somebody smiles back, we say, "Just take the low-hanging fruit." For some, that is a lot more doable.

Barry's team is self-conscious that knocking on doors can inconvenience the residents. His team always "starts with an apology: 'Thanks for opening your door.'"

"If you ask people, 'Do you have time to talk, they will say 'no.' So don't ask. That's just a tip," Janice explained to me. Instead, her team in Japan invites people to fill out surveys on their beliefs. The team also hands out energy bars to attract people and invites passersby to Christian events.

In Ireland, Ted's team went door-to-door to invite people to an event at the local hotel where there would be an evangelistic event. "I don't think I saw anyone accept the Lord at the doorstep, but at the film, we saw two become Christians. They joined a local church and are believers to this day."

> Barry's door-to-door team often involves an invitation for prayer. We ask, "Do you have anything going on in your life that you would like prayer for?" Often, they say, "No, we're fine. Thank you..." And maybe 15 or 20% of people say, "Well how nice, Yeah, I do need prayer." Generally speaking, the people with whom we have good engagement are those who are having some kind of catastrophic need: "I just got a cancer diagnosis," "I'm going through a tough divorce." Or something like that.

This sort of invitational ministry also involves inviting people to read literature. Barry explained, "We offer – always *offer*, never *tell* – *offer* to give them a tract or a gospel of John. And if they're interested, we give them my business card." A typical response is, "I'll take what you have, but I don't want to talk." One man even said, "Get away from me." And another, "I don't want to hear it." Barry said these responses are, "not a big deal. We say, 'Thank you for your time' and we move on."

Barry also explained that the planned invitational approach may also involve making people aware of support groups at the church, such as divorce care, addiction recovery, and grief support. He told me,

> We offered one man prayer, and he said, "I'm three days sober." We

said "Good news. We have a Wednesday night group with a bunch of sober alcoholics. We've seen Jesus do amazing things.

Planned Programming

Pastor Ronnie is "by nature an introvert" and found it "horrifying" to do door-to-door evangelism because he knew he "would not come to the Lord by someone coming to the door." However, Ronnie went on to describe multiple ways he has shared the gospel with strangers –largely through scheduled programs in the community.

Nearly a thousand people come each week to the basketball outreach that Ronnie's church holds in an underserved community. Ronnie described these as "front porch" ministries, because "only 10% are part of the church." The ministry team teaches basketball techniques, as well as biblical principles of sportsmanship. Then the coaches extend invitations to church. Ronnie said, "Several families have come to the basketball outreach and eventually ended up becoming part of the church."

Ronnie's church also holds block parties on public school campuses throughout the summer. "We live in a part of the country where faith and school are not compartmentalized," he explained. At the parties, they invite people to men's and women's ministries, and they disseminate Christian literature.

Planned Befriending

Two participants deliberately schedule a time to initiate friendships with strangers, in the hopes of witnessing. Janice, in Southeast Asia, explained that her long-term strategy on campus is to widen her network of friends. As Pastor Barry described above, sometimes evangelists "need more fish in the pond."

As with the planned invitations and planned programming approaches above, the planned-befriending approach takes the pressure off of budding evangelists. Janice tells new missionaries, "You don't have to share the gospel the first time. Just make a friend." In fact, this may be the perfect approach for more timid people. Janice theorized, "Introverts can have deeper conversations with people."

Planned befriending is one of the only viable approaches for Janice's context, as proselytism is highly discouraged in her host country. In fact, her organization is not permitted to work on campuses, "So you need to just make friends...Is this someone you can invest in - get to know...where are their interests?" Janice believes this approach is far more effective than randomly approaching people with a gospel presentation. She describes her model as "hands-free" evangelism: There is no Gospel app and no tracts.

They just have "normal conversations...I just want to talk to people."

Ronnie described his planned befriending at the gym, where people can be a sort of "captive audience." "Most of the conversations are about lifting weights," but he tries to initiate conversations about "having peace in your life." He told me, "Most of these conversations are one-sided, with me talking." But then Ronnie described a rich dialog with a man who enjoyed Russian literature, as Ronnie does. The fact that the Russian authors touched on themes of Christianity seemed like an in-road. "The conversation ended up lasting over seven months. He started asking questions." Eventually, the man visited a church in his area.

Planned Service

Five participants described a regularly scheduled ministry of serving the less fortunate in hopes of starting conversations about Christianity.

Mike and Kathi's ministry began when they gave a McDonald's meal to a homeless man by a bridge in a coastal Florida town. Mike then asked him if he went to church and handed him a tract. "Then it became five. Then ten," Mike recalled. "So, my wife started cooking." They now serve 200 meals a week out of their SUV. Kathi explained the people's need for this sort of help: "Some of the people we serve are felons and can't work. One had even murdered someone."

The couple takes four church members at a time to the homeless in the city. The team starts with a question: "Hey do you want some coffee?" Then they ask, "Are you a Christian? We're Christians." They read the literature along with their audience, "so they don't stick it in their pocket and forget about it." Then they offer to pray. In fact, Kathi said one man told her, "Don't let your husband leave. I need prayer." Mike said he delivers a "sermon in a second: 'God loves you; he wants to hear from you; he has a plan for you.'" The couple now holds Bible studies at the marina park. They are currently in the fifth chapter of John.

Pastor Barry and Pastor Jake both lead door-to-door teams in less fortunate neighborhoods. They ask, "Is there anything you need. Do you need groceries?" They also invite the families to church. Barry, who lived much of his life in Mexico, explained, "The only people who regularly decline to talk to us or to take our literature are those who don't speak English."

The Spontaneous Context

In addition to the five scheduled evangelism models above, participants described many spontaneous experiences where their witness included praying, inviting, proclaiming, befriending, or serving.

In preparation for our interview, Andrea (a Bible translator) told me she had multiple examples of spontaneous evangelism:

> The lady in the cave, the man on the airplane, the prisoner in the jail, the mom in spinning class, the lady at the Alpha course, the linguist, the pregnant lady, the rude man in the McDonalds, the elite professional from a world religion, the man from a restricted country who wanted the Bible, and the Peace Corps worker... and of all those, only two came to Christ. But I feel strongly about witnessing to strangers.

Andrea told me about one who came to Christ. She was in a spinning class and mentioned she was a missionary. A woman there retorted, "What about me, who will tell me about Jesus?" Andrea discovered that this woman had a great deal of pain in her life. She later looked up the woman's address and wrote her a letter outlining the good news of Jesus Christ. "I explained the gospel. I didn't hear back; but I came across her a couple of years later, sitting in a coffee shop, memorizing scriptures." They keep in touch.

Mary said she had a "boring life" being raised Christian. She asked God for her life to have a "good story." And she ended up being involved in a landmark adoption case. She now uses that story to segue into the topic that's "all in the Bible: the story about being adopted into God's family." Mary told me that a reporter from Italy said he had never heard of the notion that God adopts all of us, and he asked for her to send him all the scriptures on the subject.

JB, who systematically does proclamation ministry, also has many examples of spontaneous evangelism. Recently, he asked his waitress, "Can I pray for you?" "If they take the opportunity, I then ask them, 'Do you know for sure if you died today that you would go to heaven?'"

Steve was a union carpenter for more than thirty years and would receive new apprentices regularly. Here was his approach:

> I would ask, What is their life like? What are they attracted to? You'll hear in those stories, what they're hoping for. You're listening for dreams. What is a common ground where I can build trust...So I tune my heart to that, and the Spirit will say, "Ask them about that."

Steve specifically told me about one of his apprentices. "After a number of life experiences... two years later, he came to faith."

The Fruit of Stranger-Evangelism
The central finding of this study is that stranger evangelism contains a rich variety of experiences that are typical of any ministry. I was surprised that

participants do not monolithically conceptualize a "successful" evangelistic encounter as one that results in conversion. Participants are thrilled to be involved in any type of ministry to strangers. Barry told me, "We have never had an outing event where we didn't have at least one very positive experience." However, participants did describe a continuum of results, from rejection to interest, to conversion.

Rejection

Eight participants described experiences with rejection. Andrea mentioned that telling people she is in ministry opens opportunities to talk about religion; however, "It can also be a shutdown. I can't tell you how many people have turned away from me in the airplane when they find out what I do."

Ronnie's Bible college required door-to-door ministry. Students would return to campus to provide numbers of converts. But Ronnie referred to this portion as a "walk of shame," because, "My tally was always zero...Nobody said 'I'd like to hear more.'"

As Barry was at the gym, he engaged a man in a conversation about Jesus. "Then the man blurted out, 'People keep telling me Jesus died for my sins, but who the blankety-blank asked him to?'"

Another form of rejection involves turning-the-tables. Janice explained that sometimes starting religious conversations with Muslims has resulted in them trying to convert her. She gave a concrete example of a student from Egypt.

Three participants explained how they politely find a "way out" when they receive a negative response. Here is Jake's description:

> It's understanding non-verbal cues. One kid pretended to be talking on the phone [to avoid having to talk to Jake]. I said, "I'm not going to push you – if you want to read this tract later, go ahead and read it." And most people will see that I'm being respectful and will say, "Yeah, I'll read it."

Interest

People often appreciate the invitation for prayer. Barry says people "are surprised anyone is out canvassing, offering prayer.... They are not interested in an unsolicited message, but are interested in having someone ask, 'Is there anything going on in your life that we can pray for?'" A prostitute in Florida embraced Kathi and said, "I want you to hug me because you showed me true love."

Invitations to church also result in people showing interest. For example, Mike and Kathi reported that two of the street people to whom they ministered have shown up to church.

Profession of Faith
Some participants could describe specific examples of conversions as a result of their stranger-evangelism. Jake recalled how he spent half an hour with a group of teens:

> One of them felt convicted of sin and started to tear up. He said, "My gosh, if this is true, I'm in trouble." Some of his buddies were like, "This is true, man, come to church with us." He said, "I don't want to be that way anymore."

Jake described how the young man prayed to confess Christ. Jake gave him a Bible and recommended a church in the area.

While Andrea was on a Teen Missions trip in England, she met a woman who was researching religions. The woman attended one of the events and took notes on the message. She told Andrea, "That's it, I accept this. I believe it. I want to be a Christian." Andrea kept in touch with her for the past 20 years. "She led her family and others to Christ."

Over a thousand people prayed to receive the Lord due to JB's metropolitan ministry. "I can't be sure that they were all converted but some were. One went into the Anglican ministry." JB described a woman from Moscow who prayed to receive the Lord, came back months later with "10 or 12 more friends from Russia," and six prayed to receive Christ. "I kept in touch with that woman for years. She was definitely converted."

Ronnie has seen two prostitutes from the neighborhood come to their church over the years. "One leads one of the women's ministries now."

Blessings for the Evangelist
Stranger-evangelism also results in blessings for the heralds themselves. Barry referred to his small team that continues to do door-to-door visits. "They haven't been as discouraged as you might think." In fact, Barry believes God has blessed his church for making the effort. "You go to forty doors, strike out every time; then on Tuesday God sends you someone you never thought would come to your office, and you lead him to Christ."

JB expressed the same sentiment: "God has blessed our church because we were unashamed to bring the gospel to the streets."

Such ministry can be contagious. Mike explained that his initiative inspired others in his congregation to start similar ministries.

Discussion and Implications

Below I will discuss how participants' experiences relate to the biblical and scholarly literature on befriending, overcoming awkwardness, the power differential, and the impact on the herald.

Befriending

The participants were not monolithically taking on the role of herald. In addition to servants, some were genuinely interested in befriending people, and in understanding their religious backgrounds. Vanderwerf (2018) surveyed Minnesota poker players to understand their experiences with evangelism. In contrast to the "transactional" approach (where churches offer a free event for the community in exchange for an opportunity to present the gospel), he suggests (based on participant data) that Christians engage in "learner evangelism." Genuinely asking about another's faith can lead to rich conversations. Camphouse (2010) uses a similar moniker, "listening-based evangelism," that also involves a humble bid toward understanding the other.

Researchers should design quantitative studies from the perspective of the recipients of evangelism, to see how they perceive befriending differing from door-to-door efforts.

Overcoming Awkwardness

Approaching strangers to talk about Jesus can be socially awkward. Participants described disrupting people's dates at the beach, their weekend plans, or their personal space. Goffman (1971) referred to these sorts of disruptions as invasions of the "territories of the self." Specifically, talking with strangers about their religious views invades their personal space and the right to control conversation and information (Ingram, 1989, p. 20). Communication theorists refer to this breach of boundaries as a "norm expectancy violation" (Burgoon & Jones, 1976). Socially "normal" people would not deliberately invade another person's space — as it would dishonor the other. However, participants' descriptions above indicate that many of their encounters — whether spontaneous or planned — cannot be "intrusive" (to use Ingram's term above) if the Holy Spirit planned such meetings. Several authors have noted that heralds trust that it is the Holy Spirit – not the evangelist – who transgresses "territories of the self" to reveal God to people through evangelistic encounters (Ingram, 1989, p. 21; Smith, 2011, p. 96).

Many evangelistic ministries have worked out strategies to overcome the awkwardness: Asking people to participate in surveys, handing out candy bars or tracts, inviting people to events, and even offering prayer are all less threatening acts than approaching people to ask about their religious beliefs. Ingram's (1989) discussion of Cru's strategies made a similar point: Public activities that are more familiar (like surveys) can be a bridge to the more awkward activity of witnessing (p. 22).

Participants have also discovered that they invade fewer "territories of the self" if they approach strangers in a "third place" (Oldenburg, 1989) where they, and the evangelee, belong. Third places are where people spend time between home (their "first place") and work (their "second place"). Such places include health clubs, campuses, and parks — the sorts of places where participants said they engaged in planned and spontaneous evangelism.

Not all participants showed the same degree of emotional intelligence when it comes to overcoming awkwardness. Some clearly knew stranger-evangelism is invasive, and they had strategies for mitigating the awkwardness. Others did not address the issue. Further research is needed to see if self-confidence and emotional intelligence are correlated with engagement in stranger evangelism. Dunaetz (2019) has noted that Christians may shy away from sharing the gospel due to the "mum effect" — a fear of the consequences of sharing news that may be received harshly. He suggests that while all church members may be fit for engaging in outreach, the task of evangelism may be more suitable for those who can navigate the mum effect with finesse. In any case, evangelistic ministries would benefit from debriefing all their workers on the ways they experienced (and overcame) awkwardness.

It would be helpful to have a longitudinal study on people's perceptions of "being witnessed to" to see how attitudes are changing. Such knowledge could shape further efforts in stranger-evangelism.

Mitigating the Power Differential

Participants clearly want all "strangers" to know about Jesus Christ. Many, though, often discuss matters of faith with those who are not only strangers but are different from themselves (participants discussed reaching poorer communities, youth, the homeless, and those who are from ethnic backgrounds other than their own). Some recognized that being "different" helps catch others' attention. But in many of these cases, "difference" also involved a power differential (e.g., participants may be older or far wealthier than those they are trying to reach).

Ethicist Elmer Thiessen (2018) noted that when evangelism involves a power differential, the act may not only transgress social boundaries but ethical ones. For example, some see it as emotionally manipulative for youth leaders to persuade young people to be baptized on the last night of a youth retreat, for a teacher in a public school to use classroom time to defend the Christian faith, or for church planters in the least developed countries to "buy converts" with gifts of rice. Thiessen does not wish for Christians to cease their work of evangelism; rather, he encourages evangelists to plan out their interactions in a way that allows for individuals' autonomy in how they will respond.

Evangelicals seem to be shifting away from evangelism, at least partially due to concerns about the ethics of persuading people to convert. Whereas 96% of millennial Christians agreed or strongly agreed that "part of my faith means being a witness about Jesus," 47% agreed or strongly agreed that "it is wrong to share one's personal beliefs with someone of a different faith in hopes that they will" convert (Barna Group, 2019, p. 47).

Several participants were clearly aware of the importance of "autonomy." They politely found "an out" when their audience was uninterested. They also described "dropping the bait." If their audience did not take the bait, they often did not push the topic. There is strong scriptural support for this posture toward the other. While Jesus was confrontational at times (Luke 11:37-54), when he was specifically engaged in ministry, he paid attention to the needs and interests of those he was serving. For example, he asked Bartimaeus, "What do you want me to do for you?" (Mark 10:51, NIV). He responded to Jairus' need (Mark 5:21-43), and he allowed the rich young ruler to walk away (Mark 10:27-27).

Stranger-evangelism raises not only ethical issues but also legal ones. The participant who worked in a Southeast Asian country could only engage in "planned-befriending" evangelism. There are also potential legal issues in the USA. For example, when the Todd Becker Foundation was planning a rally on drunk driving, word got out that the organization would end the evening with an altar call. Boston (2010) referred to this bait-and-switch tactic as "Stealth evangelism." The civil rights group Americans United put pressure on the local school district to make sure no religious conversionary talk would be involved.

Overt evangelism among strangers is foundational to a sense of religious freedom in the USA. The Supreme Court heard a case from Ohio on "doorbell evangelism" and determined that the right must be protected as part of free speech ("Doorbell evangelism," 2002). But Christians also engage in evangelism in many countries where they are not legally allowed to initiate conversionary conversations with strangers.

Impact on the Herald

The impact of stranger-evangelism on the spiritual lives of the evangelists was a minor focus in this study. Ko (2015) predicted the effect that cold-call evangelism would have on the team that engages in such a work. He said it would increase one's prayer life, make one more attuned to the needs of others, and may even result in conversions.

Scripture teaches that proclamation is a spiritual activity—one where the Triune God infills the herald. We experience God's presence and assistance as we declare what God has done (Luke 12:12; John 14:26; Rom. 8:26).

The findings section explained that stranger-evangelism efforts can be "contagious." Such innovation in lay ministry was the theme of Greear's (2016) *Gaining by Losing.* He argues that the church exists to help people discover their gifts and passions, and to empower them to use those gifts in their communities.

Conclusion

Stranger-evangelism is alive and well. Yet it cannot be reductionistically characterized by the trope of two nicely dressed people knocking on doors in an effort to persuade people to convert. Table 2 below shows the richness of ministries that Christians are engaging in with strangers.

Table 2: *Types of Stranger-Evangelism*

Planned Proclamation	Approach: A "hook" (tracts, candy bars, Starbucks cards, an optical illusion, a quick survey) Action: Explaining the problem of sin and the good news of the judicial atonement
Planned Invitations	Approach: Apology for the inconvenience Action: Offering prayer, tangible needs, invitation to church or church's ministries
Planned Programming	Approach: Community program (basketball, block parties, after school programs) Action: Invitation to church's ministries; offering literature
Planned befriending	Approach: A bid to know the other (coffee, party, camp, survey) Action: Willingness to understand the other's interests and beliefs; movement at their pace
Planned Service	Approach: Tangible needs (food for the homeless, etc.) Action: Invitation to church, Bible study
Spontaneous Stranger-Evangelism	Approach: Listening to the other Action: Responding to the other's need with prayer, encouragement, or literature

Understanding the multiple approaches above has helped to mitigate some of my own fears of stranger-evangelism. Because it is a ministry that includes a rich set of approaches and actions, there seems to be space for all Christians to get involved.

References

Abrahamse, J. M. (2021). God's marketeer: Changing perceptions of Billy Graham's 1954 crusade in the Dutch media. *European Journal of Theology, 30*(2), 312–344.

Aldrich, J. C. (1983). Lifestyle evangelism: Winning through winsomeness. *Christianity Today, 27*(1):12-17.

Berger, R. (2013). Now I see it, now I don't: Researcher's position and reflexivity in qualitative research. *Qualitative Research, 15*(2), 219–234. https://doi:10.1177/1468794112468475

Barna Group. (2019). *Reviving evangelism.* Barna Group

Beougher, T. (2005). "The Great Commission and personal evangelism." In Chuck Lawless and Thom S. Rainer, (eds.) *The challenge of the Great Commission: Essays on God's mandate for the local church,* (pp. 121-136). Pinnacle.

Birt, L., Scott, S., Cavers, D., Campbell, C., & Walter, F. (2016). Member checking: A tool to enhance trustworthiness or merely a nod to validation? *Qualitative Health Research, 26*(13), 1802–1811. https://doi.org/10.1177/1049732316654870

Boston, B. (2010). Stealth evangelism and the public schools. *Education Digest: Essential Readings Condensed for Quick Review, 76*(3), pp. 40–43.

Burgoon, J. & Jones, S. (1976). Toward a theory of personal space expectations and their violations. *Human Communication Research, 2*(2), 131-146. https://doi.org/10.1111/j.1468-2958.1976.tb00706.x

Camphouse, A. C. (2010). *Godbearing in practice: Developing spiritual midwifery through listening-based evangelism.* [Doctoral dissertation, Claremont School of Theology].

Coleman, R. (1993). *The Master plan of evangelism.* Revell.

Dunaetz, D. R. (2019). Evangelism, social media, and the mum effect. *Evangelical Review of Theology, 43*(2), 138-151.

Goffman, E. (1971). *Relations in public.* Harper Torchbooks.

Greear, J. D. (2016). *Gaining by losing: Why the future belongs to churches that send.* Grand Rapids, MI: Zondervan.

Grudem, W. (1994). *Systematic theology: An introduction to biblical doctrine.* Grand Rapids, MI: Zondervan.

Ingram, L. C. (1989). Evangelism as frame intrusion: Observations on witnessing in public places. *Journal for the Scientific Study of Religion, 28*(1), 17–26. https://doi.org/10.2307/1387249

Johnston, T. (2007). *Charts for a theology of evangelism.* B&H Academic.

Ko, P. (2015). "Why you should go cold turkey." https://au.thegospelcoalition.org/article/why-you-should-go-cold-turkey/

Moody, L. E. (1983). Putting lifestyle evangelism to work. *Christianity Today*, *27*(1), 14.

Oldenburg, R. (1989). *The Great good place: Cafes, coffee shops, community centers, beauty parlors, general stores, bars, hangouts, and how they get you through the day. Paragon House.*

Saldaña, J. (2015). *The coding manual for qualitative researchers.* Sage.

Saxton, K. (2017). *Family ministry and evangelism: An empirical study of family ministry engagement and baptism ratios in the Southern Baptist* Convention. [Doctoral dissertation, Southern Baptist Theological Seminary].

Schmidt, H. J. (1990). Crusade decisions: Counting and accounting for lost sheep. *Journal of the American Society for Church Growth, 1*(1), 16-35.

Skidmore, D. (1986). "Double amputee completes cross-country odyssey." *AP News.* https://apnews.com/article/a1675fac4bc7b63d9d95140611fe5521

Simpson, M. (2003). *Permission evangelism: When to talk, when to walk.* NexGen.

Smith, S. (2011). *T4T: A discipleship rerevolution.* WIGTake Resources.

Thiessen, E. (2018). *The Scandal of evangelism: A biblical study of the ethics of evangelism.* Cascade.

Vanderwerf, FSE. (2018). *Embracing learner evangelism: Bar poker community insights for Minnesota United Methodists.* [Doctoral dissertation, Asbury Theological Seminary].

Whitam, F. L. (1966). *Adolescence and mass persuasion: A study of teen-age decision-making at a Billy Graham crusade.* [Doctoral dissertation, Indiana University].

About the Author

Kenneth Nehrbass, Ph.D., is an anthropology and translation consultant with the Summer Institute of Linguistics and is the Director of Special Projects at California Baptist University.

GREAT COMMISSION
RESEARCH JOURNAL
2022, Vol. 14(2) 65-84

Forming Saints in a Digital Context

Mark Teasdale

Garrett Evangelical Seminary

Abstract

Biblical and scholarly sources agree on the importance of forming Christians to seek after holy living to make them more effective evangelists, such that the ministries of evangelism and spiritual formation are intertwined. They also agree that one of the primary roles of the church is to provide for this formation. However, the practices for doing this have been complicated by the heavy move toward digital ministry because of COVID-19. Congregations can continue this formational work even in highly digital contexts by helping Christians tell their story through lifelogging, providing rituals and disciplines to sanctify time and physical spaces, and equipping Christians for evangelistic mission.

I was raised to believe that evangelism was defined as bringing someone to assent intellectually to a series of propositional truths about Jesus and certain scriptural teachings. In my home congregation, Bible memorization, beginning in first grade Sunday school and continuing through high school, factored heavily into preparing us for this. It was most fully manifested in our confirmation class, which entailed a careful exposition of the tract "The Four Spiritual Laws" by our youth pastor. Our final exam in the class, which we had to pass to be confirmed, entailed reciting the entirety of the tract from memory, including the laws themselves and the supporting Bible verses for each one. I'm proud to say that I passed and was confirmed at the age of fourteen.

As fastidious as our youth pastor was in making certain that we knew the Four Spiritual Laws, one thing he forgot to do was to ask if we had all been baptized, a requirement for confirmation in The United Methodist Church. My parents, who lived in rural Washington State when I was born, had approached the pastor of the church where they had been married to see if he would perform the baptism. He refused on the grounds that they were not members (my mother was raised a Baptist and the church was Episcopalian, so the idea of joining was a non-starter). So, my parents took me to a nearby field and prayed over me. As my mother explained to me years later, they had dedicated me to God, figured that was good enough, and forgot about baptism. My sister came along a little over a year later and they did the same thing.

Returning to my teenage years: A year after I was confirmed, my sister was going through confirmation. This time, the senior pastor visited the class and asked if everyone had been baptized. She said no, and he replied that they would need to baptize her during the confirmation service. She asked why, since they had confirmed her older brother the previous year and *he* was not baptized.

And so it was that at the age of fifteen, a year after I was confirmed, I was baptized at Mt. Oak UMC in Mitchelville, Maryland. In the United Methodist Church, this is considered a significant breach of sacramental theology because baptism and confirmation are understood as sequential in coming to faith. Infant baptism represents the grace of God welcomed on the infant's behalf through the faith of the family and congregation. They promise to raise the child in this faith so that, in time, the child can confirm that faith by publicly professing acceptance of the grace of God through Jesus Christ. Based on this theology, baptism can occur before or simultaneously with confirmation, but never after it since there is technically no faith to confirm prior to baptism.

My story may be a bit unique among Methodists, but the logic related to evangelism is not. Many Christians would agree with my youth pastor: Evangelism is defined solely as bringing the unchurched to a cognitive understanding and assent to certain Christian teachings. Once you have said "Yes" to Jesus, you are as formed as you need to be. You need to learn a bit more, adding some Bible verses and doctrines to your knowledge bank so you can articulate what you believe. You also may need to clean up your morality a bit, but that's it. After all, you've taken the biggest step by professing Christ, which guarantees your place in heaven. What more is needed other than to send you back out to share your faith with others?

This was certainly the thinking of my youth pastor. I had already publicly confessed Christ and I was memorizing what he saw as the core doctrines of the faith so I could explain them to my friends. What did baptism or any other form of formation matter? I was already secure for eternity, and I was being prepared to help others receive that assurance. This was enough.

Except, it is not. Jesus was clear that he was calling people not just to eternal glory, but to become his disciples who are baptized and who obey all he taught (Matthew 28:20) leading to a life of holiness (Matthew 5:48). This means that evangelism must entail both the invitation to follow Jesus and formational work to guide those being evangelized into a life of holiness.

One implication of this is to avoid sequencing formation after invitation. Jesus demonstrated this in how he called the disciples to follow him and accepted them as his companions and messengers even though they often lacked faith in who he was and the message he taught (Matthew 8:26, 14:31, 16:8, 17:20, 28:17). He continued to form them both in the basics of the gospel message and in holy living throughout his earthly ministry.

Evangelism and Formation in Holiness

Scholars of evangelism have been sounding the call for formation and evangelism to be linked for some time. The late William Abraham contended in *The Logic of Evangelism* that evangelism is initiating people into the Kingdom of God. This entailed forming people in six ways: 1) communally by having the people of God come alongside a person to form them, 2) intellectually through the teaching of the faith, 3) morally through instilling in them the ability to judge wisely between good and evil, 4) experientially through the process of conversion, 5) vocationally through helping them discern how to participate in the *missio Dei*, especially by helping them recognize how the Holy Spirit was moving in their lives to empower them for mission, and 6) spiritually by teaching them to commune with God through the spiritual disciplines (Abraham, 1989). While Abraham was insistent that evangelism only properly described the initiation of people into the Kingdom, Kim Reisman pointed out in her reflection on his work that this initiation was so wide-ranging that it functionally blurred the lines between the initial call to faith and discipleship formation (Reisman, 2019).

Gordon T. Smith, in *Called to Be Saints*, declared:

Evangelism is about fostering and cultivating the opportunities for a person to meet Jesus...It is not about persuading them of certain truths or laws, or even about believing that Jesus has done something—that if they "believe" it will lead to their "salvation." It is rather about meeting Christ Jesus in person and in real time (Smith, 2014).

Having met Jesus, Smith contends that we must continue to be formed by "fostering the capacity, the orientation, the discipline of living in union with Christ" (Smith, 2014, p.58) until we reach spiritual maturity. We demonstrate this maturity by being wise, doing good work, loving others, and being happy (Smith, 2014). Again, while the initial work of evangelism is technically separate from formation, Smith blurs the boundaries between the two because the goal is not conversion, but leading people to maturity as they relate to Jesus.

Rick Richardson, whose book *Reimagining Evangelism* presents evangelism as a relational journey with others rather than as a single, high-pressure sales pitch, agrees with this.

> Our model of conversion has pushed us to draw lines in order to figure out who's in and who's out, and we look for a one-time event, a decision, that distinguishes people on the outside from those on the inside. I don't know about you, but for me this constant attempt to figure out who has become a Christian and who's in and who's out has been a very frustrating and fruitless experience. The new model, a model based on the image of a journey, sees all of us moving either toward the goal or away from the goal. If the goal is to be a wholehearted follower of Jesus, then we are at different points along the way. But the crucial question is whether we are moving toward the center and beginning to follow in the footsteps of the Leader (Richardson, 2006, p. 18).

Beth Seversen in her book *Not Done Yet* provides empirical evidence for the wisdom of avoiding hard lines between evangelism and discipleship formation. Having collected and analyzed the data from churches that are successfully both attracting and retaining young adults, she writes, "Many young adults are retained at church *before* they are evangelized, and others are retained *simultaneously* as they are being evangelized" (Seversen, 2020, p. 152).

She even observes that these churches go as far as developing young adults as leaders before the young adults become Christians. They do this for two reasons: First, it shows that the church loves young adults enough to invest in them. Second, it allows young adults to claim ownership of the church's ministries. This provides the young adults greater reason to remain integrated with the Christian community and, for some of them, to convert to the Christian faith if they have not already (Seversen, 2020).

The integration of evangelism and discipleship formation is also present in the ministry of Saint Paul. Acts 24:25 records that while he was imprisoned in Caesarea, "Paul talked [to Governor Felix] about righteousness, self-control and the judgment to come" (NIV). In his discourse, Paul moves seamlessly between topics meant to encourage Felix to decide to follow Christ and topics about how Felix could be formed as a Christian disciple. Beyond this, Paul's missionary journeys and letters provide a mixture of presenting the gospel message for people to receive and exhortations for them to be formed in the image of Christ in their knowledge, character, ethics, and relationships. Consider how many times Paul pauses in his letters to express his prayers and desires for the recipients to grasp and then grow in the gospel.

All of this reinforces what we saw in Jesus' ministry with the disciples: Evangelism and discipleship are not a linear sequence but are intermingled. We simultaneously are calling people to decide to follow Jesus and to enter a process of sanctification. While these activities may be technically or heuristically separated, they naturally occur alongside each other on the frontlines of ministry. Consequently, it seems God was far less concerned with the order of my baptism and confirmation than The United Methodist Church would have been!

Forming Evangelists in the Church

A necessary corollary to this is that the effectiveness of evangelism is more dependent on the character of the evangelist than the practices the evangelist deploys. This helps explain why Jesus never stops forming his disciples. As his messengers, the lives they lead will speak as loudly as their message. For example, when Jesus sends out the Twelve, he tells them, "As you enter the home, give it *your* greeting. If the home is deserving, let *your* peace rest on it; if it is not, let *your* peace return to you" (Matthew 10:12-13 NIV, italics added). It is the character of peace the disciples bring with them that adorns their message.

The importance of the evangelist's character is further supported by psychological research into the factors that help people accept feedback on their behavior, such as during an annual performance evaluation. Psychologists have determined that "the Source [i.e., the person providing the feedback] is the face of the feedback and therefore is inherently entangled with the recipient's perception and experience of the feedback event…[T]he feedback source may be the most important factor in whether the recipient accepts the feedback" (Gregory & Levy, 2015, p. 47). The implication of this is clear: our best strategy for effective evangelism is to focus on forming Christians as holy disciples.

This goes a step beyond the current ubiquitous call for evangelists to be "authentic." The call to authenticity is to avoid the trap of Christians thinking they must have all the answers or have a polished, professional presentation in order to share the gospel with others. The unchurched are far less concerned about these niceties than they are with interacting with a real person in a genuine way, even if that person is fallible (Richardson, 2006).

Given that the evangelist is the "face of the message," we need to ask: What is the character of the Christian who is being authentic? We all know people who loudly proclaim their Christian faith, but are authentically unpleasant, misanthropic, and rude. The need is for Christians who are not just authentic, but who are authentically seeking holiness. Christians would share the gospel through word, deed, and lifestyle, as well as demonstrate it in their being (Robert, 2022).

This call to holiness requires individual Christians to be intentional about their formation as disciples of Jesus Christ. It also requires a greater role for the church because it is within the church that Christians are formed in holiness.

Paul was clear that God intended the church to bring people into spiritual maturity:

> So Christ himself gave the apostles, the prophets, the evangelists, the pastors and teachers, to equip his people for works of service, so that the body of Christ may be built up until we all reach unity in the faith and in the knowledge of the Son of God and become mature, attaining to the whole measure of the fullness of Christ (Ephesians 4:11-13, NIV).

Whether we follow Alan Hirsch in reading this in terms of APEST (the five ministry roles of Apostle, Prophet, Evangelist, Shepherd, and Teacher) or not, the overall point is clear: Jesus works through the church to form people as his disciples who are part of his mission. This has been borne out in Christian history and scholarship.

Some of the best historical examples are John and Charles Wesley. They found that it was impossible for most people to seek after holiness apart from being an active member of a community of believers who were dedicated to growing in grace. They observed trenchantly, "'Holy solitaries' is a phrase no more consistent with the gospel than holy adulterers. The gospel of Christ knows of no religion, but social; no holiness but social holiness" (Wesley et. al., 1739). This conviction led especially John to become one of the most successful small group organizers in evangelical history. A great many small group ministry structures today utilize a version of the structures he built for drawing people into Christian community and formation.

Two of the scholars we have already considered, William Abraham and Gordon Smith, affirm the importance of the church's role in discipleship formation. For Abraham, the church was essential for establishing the canon of divine revelation that disclosed a faithful and accurate rendering of how people ought to live as disciples of Jesus Christ. In addition, the church provided a wide array of tools to immerse people in that canon so they could be formed in Christ's image (Abraham, 1989). These tools overlap with the four broad activities Smith contends congregations must offer to form people in holiness: liturgical worship, teaching and learning, missional outreach, and spiritual direction and pastoral care (Smith, 2014).

James Wilhoit, in his book *Spiritual Formation as if the Church Mattered*, states that "spiritual formation takes place best in and through community" (Wilhoit, 2008). To this end, he lays out a curriculum for spiritual formation in community that entails four aspects: receiving, remembering, responding, and relating. We receive both the news that we are broken sinners and the good news that God's grace comes through Jesus to heal us. We remember by being constantly called back to our need for God's grace so that we are not tempted to begin believing in our self-sufficiency or in the power of anything other than Christ to heal us. We respond by sharing the grace we have received with others through acts of service. We relate by being vulnerable and open to others in the Christian community (Wilhoit, 2008). He then provides practical ways that local churches can offer this fourfold curriculum.

There are many other historical examples and scholars that could be cited. In an attempted synthesis, I propose the following three broad areas of activity the church needs to provide to form Christians in holiness so they can be effective evangelists:

1. Immersion in the Christian story in such a way that Christians can articulate their personal stories as part of the full salvation narrative found in Scripture.
2. Rituals and disciplines that help Christians recognize, receive, and grow in God's grace both personally and corporately.
3. Equipping Christians to share the grace of God with others in the world.

I have developed these three areas with an eye toward their practicability.

It should be relatively easy for local congregations to develop ministries that fit into each. Indeed, the texts we have reviewed are full of practical suggestions on this score, as is a small mountain of publications, blogs, and YouTube videos that deal with spiritual formation. However, with the advent of COVID-19 and the ensuing quarantines, many of these practices were suddenly rendered impossible because physically gathering was no longer an option. In its place, nearly every aspect of Christian ministry shifted to a digital format. This raises the question: Can the church form people in holiness in a digital context? Can it help shape digital saints?

Digital Saints

The impact of the shift to digital ministry was an earthquake for most congregations, especially more traditional congregations that understood their role primarily around gathering in a particular way to carry out particular practices. A cottage industry sprang up nearly overnight to study this impact and to offer thoughts on how to operate in this new situation—a situation that now seems unlikely to recede. Even with the current capacity of congregations to gather in person while following certain protocols, the forced shift to digital ministry has left a permanent impression on how Christian communities are likely to operate from this point forward. Moreover, the ever-present threat of new virus variants means that the potential for having in-person gatherings restricted again is a real possibility.

Publications and reports that have sought to address this new digital reality for churches have broadly fallen into two categories. The first category has focused on cataloging how congregations have responded, some congregations trying to replicate the in-person experience online and some reimagining their ministries entirely to take advantage of the new digital platform. The second category has sought to help congregations make the change from replication to reimagination.

This latter category of resources is similar to the resources on digital pedagogy. Those of us who teach could just try to replicate the in-person classroom or we could do a deep dive into what our course objectives are and learn the new tools and possibilities for achieving those objectives using a digital platform. These resources are likewise helping congregations reflect on the nature of the church and introducing congregations to the capabilities that a digital environment offers for their ministries.

What I have not seen is a resource that asks the question that brings together the question of formation and digital ministry. Is it possible for congregations to help form saints in a digital environment? I believe that it is, with an important caveat.

The caveat is that we need to avoid bifurcating how we think about digital and in-person experiences. In earlier scholarship, this separation has been allowed based on the extent to which individuals were comfortable relating theology to technology. Phil Meadows suggested three categories: 1) "digital alien" for those who were most critical of how digital activity could threaten "authentic Christian discipleship and community," 2) "digital pioneer" for those willing to adopt digital tools insofar as they could be used for Christian ends, and 3) "digital native" for those who accept that discipleship formation occurs equally digitally and in-person (Meadows, 2012). While Meadows' categories are helpful reminders of the spectrum of responses people in the church have toward digital technology, they are premised on the notion that there is a separation between "authentic" Christian ministry done in-person and digital ministry. The church must recognize and address the fact that for a wide swath of people outside of their congregations, there is no longer a separation between "real life" and "digital life." There is simply real life, which includes and values both a person's in-person and digital activities. Accordingly, the church must be a "digital native" while not ignoring the ethical mandate to reflect on the effects of digital technology on Christian community per the "digital alien" nor the entrepreneurial spirit of the "digital pioneer."

Ending this bifurcation is more than just making a mental shift, it is acknowledging the way that technology has already moved. The internet is no longer confined only to computers, phones, and tablets. It is an "internet of things" that allow our ovens, washing machines, dryers, thermostats, cars, and any number of other devices to be digitally connected (Meadows, 2012). Even our bodies can be digitally enhanced through prosthetics and devices that improve our hearing or sight (Meadows, 2012). Just as the internet itself is reaching out to have an impact on the physical world, so our ministries must entail forming people holistically, including digitally and in person (Beck et. al., 2021). This should be good news to many congregations. It means that they do not need to abandon their in-person ministry. Indeed, without it, their digital ministry will not be sufficient. By the same token, they must account for the digital ramifications of their in-person ministries.

In what follows, I would like to offer a modest proposal for how a congregation can form Christians in holiness so they can be more effective evangelists. Using both digital and in-person ministries that take the impact of the digital on people's lives seriously, especially when the digital predominates (such as during lockdowns), I believe congregations can offer ministries that fulfill the three areas I proposed earlier. Along with ministries that address these three areas, I would add a fourth item to consider how congregations can be held accountable for staying faithful in this work.

The ways that a congregation can fulfill the three areas needed to form Christians in holiness are:

1. Immersion in the Christian story of salvation in a way that people can find their personal stories in it through prompting people to create and share a **lifelog of their digital activities.**
2. Rituals and disciplines that help people recognize, receive, and grow in God's grace by **marking the passage of time and creating sacred space.**
3. Equipping Christians to share the grace of God in the world by helping them **re-discern their spiritual gifts and providing them opportunities to share those gifts.**
4. For the congregation to hold itself accountable, I propose **establishing new metrics that measure whether the congregation is being effective in its work of forming people in holiness.**

Immersion in the Christian Story through Lifelogging

I borrow the idea of "lifelogging" from Doug Estes. In his book SimChurch, Estes describes the practice of lifelogging as "the capture, storage, and distribution of everyday experiences and information for objects and people" (Estes, 2009). This is a practice common on the internet, where, for example, companies deploy algorithms to track what sites we have visited so they can target specific ads to our browsers. Our digital life is "logged" by their tracking software to make this possible. Another example is how people "log" their lives through their posts on their various social media accounts, sharing updates about their activities, meals, places they have traveled, people they have met, and general likes and dislikes.

Estes suggests that Christians should commandeer this lifelogging process because "in contrast to the real world, the virtual world typically allows the average person to demonstrate their faithfulness in a much more consistent way, a way that is demonstrable to others" (Estes, 2009). This lifelog is visible to others in a variety of ways. In the case of social media, for example, other people can read, watch, and/or listen to everything that the Christian chooses to post, giving the Christian's social media followers immediate evidence as to whether the Christian's digital presence demonstrates holiness. Since these posts often include references to a person's activities, social media also allows people to assess if the Christian is demonstrating holiness in how they physically interact with the world.

And, while not as visible to a broader audience, the history of what people have searched on the internet and the web pages they have visited is saved by their internet service provider (ISP). In the United States, the Electronic Communications Transactional Records Act of 1996 mandates that an ISP must save all internet activity of their customers going back at least ninety days. This remains even if someone deletes their browser history on their personal computer. Even if this is never specifically tapped for others to see, it is a definitive electronic marker for whether a Christian is pursuing holiness through digital technology.

By being intentional about being gracious, sharing about our faith appropriately in online forums, engaging lovingly with others rather than giving way to the torrent of outrage so commonly found in social media and comments, and being careful about what sites we actually go to on the internet, we can create a lifelog that provides empirical evidence that we are leading holy lives. This will stand out because it is so easy to explore sin in the digital world, and our intentionality to be lights, rather than to skulk in the darkness, will demonstrate authentic holiness in our character.

To maintain such holiness in our lifelogs is no small feat, requiring a character that demonstrates the fruits of the Spirit (Galatian 5:22-23) in a way that flows into our digital activities—something that can be hard to do given the relative anonymity and sense of disconnectedness that the internet can provide us. A local congregation can help Christians with formation related to their lifelogs in two ways: First, through teaching the basics of how to engage with the digital world. Especially for young people, one of the struggles is simply to discern what good and evil look like on the internet since all of it is depicted on the same screen. Training people in theological ethics related to digital engagement is crucial and practical, and it should start at an early age. This is an act of immersing people into the Christian story in a way that fits with our new context (Dotzman, 2020).

A second way would be to offer regular accountability (which could be conducted in-person or online) through small group gatherings. In these gatherings, group members would share their lifelogs with each other by reviewing each other's social media posts and web histories. Just as it is best for us to share our verbal testimonies in church as well as sharing with the unchurched, so it is important to invite other Christians to see how we are comporting ourselves online. We need to be vulnerable to one another, letting even the secret sins become visible, both to avoid sin and to improve our ability to share our faith digitally.

These accountability groups would not only help Christians maintain holiness individually, but they would also allow Christians to demonstrate how they are a loving community. By reviewing what each other was posting on social media and searching for on the internet, group members would be able to see if any of their number was facing struggles mentally, emotionally, financially, or in any other way. This would be especially important during quarantines and lockdowns when in-person opportunities for meeting are curtailed while the potential for damage to mental health, relationships, and job security all increase. Having a community that cares enough to recognize these challenges and then step in to "carry each other's burdens" (Galatians 6:2, NIV) would not only strengthen each individual but provide an example to the larger world of how a Christian community meets the needs of the whole person. While it would be important to keep much of the information shared in this group confidential, group members could and should at least share publicly how the group had been a source of ongoing love and support for them. This would be a witness to how seeking after holiness is not just about pursuing personal moral perfection but loving one's neighbor.

Rituals and Traditions to Create Sacred Time and Space

Caring for people holistically leads us to the next item: providing rituals to mark time and space as sacred. One of the effects of the isolation caused by spending days being alone with our screens is feeling like we have entered a time warp. Many of us experienced this, especially after the quarantines in 2020. All the traditional cultural markers of the seasons passing – the Macy's Thanksgiving Day Parade, the festive holiday parties, the summer vacations, and going back to school – just evaporated away, replaced by unchanging glowing rectangles in front of us. Especially for those of us in basement offices with no window even to see the sunlight, time became a complete blur. When we reemerged after twelve or more months, we felt a bit like Rip Van Winkle waking up from his hundred-year nap. We knew time had passed, but somehow that seemed inconceivable because of the long days of everything seeming to stay the same.

Historically, churches have been a central cultural actor in marking the passage of time. Christmas and Easter services are the best-known examples of this, but the church has a rich calendar that is forged around the gospel story—Advent for the Incarnation, Christmas for the Nativity, Lent for the earthly ministry of Christ, Holy Week for the Passion of Christ, Easter for the Resurrection, Pentecost for the commissioning of the church in the power of the Holy Spirit. The church has an entire logic and set of rituals that mark time by calling people to remember salvation history.

In the same way, the church has rituals that mark and sanctify physical space. By constructing church buildings, hallowing cemeteries, and establishing camps and retreat centers, Christians mark out geographic locations that were recognized as places where human life and the Kingdom of Heaven connect by encouraging us to reflect on God being present with us and respond in faith and obedience. The rituals around both sacred times and spaces anchor the human sense that we are part of something bigger, that our lives are ordered even when our daily activities have become monotonous and mundane.

When people feel cut off from sacred time and space because their ability to connect with other Christians in person has been limited, the church needs to step in and help them recognize that the Holy Trinity is not restricted by human movement. One way it can do this is by providing new rituals and practices that help them reclaim sacred time and space even if they are at home. In doing this, the church can provide them with a practical means for bringing order and formation to their lives again. This would be a blessing both to those who are already Christians as they strive after holiness and to those who are not Christians but still yearn for a sense of order in their lives.

This would not be an unprecedented move by the church. When the circuit riders entered the "Wild West" in the late nineteenth century, one of the first things they did was to establish ritual times and places so that the frontiersmen, cowboys, prospectors, and other people who thought they had left Christianity behind could recognize the sacred again (Teasdale, 2014). Sometimes this meant commandeering a saloon for an impromptu hymn-sing and preaching service. Sometimes it meant hastily constructing a sod building to serve as a church. Almost always it meant setting up a rhythm of weekly worship and annual events on Christian holy days.

The church now faces a new digital frontier with the same post-Christian context the Wild West had to offer. Congregations can help Christians navigate this new frontier by giving them ways to remember that time and space can still be made holy, even if the space is within their personal dwelling places. How a congregation does this should be consistent with the congregation's theology. An Eastern Orthodox congregation might provide icons and candles to set up in a room, a Roman Catholic congregation might provide a crucifix. Protestants might borrow from the account of how God commanded Moses to consecrate and dedicate the tabernacle altar (Exodus 40:10, Leviticus 8:11, Numbers 7) by providing oil and prayer to consecrate a specific room (or even part of a room) as a place to engage in personal devotions and participate in regular digital worship services. The congregation can remind its members that God is present there because God can and will sanctify any space yielded to Him. Likewise, the congregation can offer morning and evening prayers that can be read, listened to online, or participated in spontaneously together with other Christians via zoom, Advent or Lenten workbooks for children to use, worshipful music to play during a time the Christian should center their thoughts on Christ, or other ways of sanctifying time. These could be available both to Christians in the congregation and those outside the congregation who need to have a sense that their time is not being lost, but redeemed.

The goal of providing sacred time and space for Christians in their dwelling places is to help them grow in their spiritual discipline. The idea is not to tame the sacred by shrinking it to being one more household item but to transfigure the mundane times and spaces that Christians inhabit. These sacred times and spaces provide regular reminders to enter God's presence with prayer, Scripture, worship, and song, both individually and corporately. The digital connections sustained by the congregation help Christians strive after holiness in their daily lives by making their homes holy places and their days holy times.

This kind of mixed digital and physical way of forming people in holiness also accorded well with the work that many congregations felt called to provide their members early in the quarantines. According to a survey conducted of churches affiliated with Exponential, the two top priorities for congregational leaders during the opening days of the pandemic were "weekend services" and "church membership care" (MacDonald et. al., 2020). In at least one instance, this was replicated outside the United States. In tracking Avonsleigh Baptist Church in Auckland, New Zealand throughout the pandemic, Lynne Maree Taylor found that the congregational leaders initially put their top priority on connecting with existing members in order to promote their spiritual, mental, social, and physical well-being (Taylor, 2021).

More than just providing a foundation for personal growth in holiness as well as stability for mental health, this sort of ministry opens the door for congregations to be an evangelistic witness to others. According to Taylor, the pattern that emerged in her case study of a congregation that was innovative digitally during the pandemic was one of experimentation leading to amplification and connection (Taylor, 2021). As the congregation experimented with digital tools to provide ministries to care for existing members, it developed new platforms that amplified those ministries such that they could connect to a much larger audience of people. The result was the initial move to help provide stability and spiritual growth for their members becoming a means for the congregation to present the gospel to far more people.

Launch People in Mission

Having established ministries that help form Christians as those who are authentically seeking after holiness and providing them with tools to demonstrate this with their lifelogs and rituals, the last step is for congregations to launch Christians on evangelistic mission. This includes both helping them recognize where they are best equipped to be in mission and creating opportunities for that mission.

The Bible is clear that God has provided gifts to his church (Romans 12:6-8, 1 Corinthians 12, Ephesians 4:7-13, Hebrews 2:4). These gifts are bestowed on individual Christians for the common good of the church and the advancement of its participation in Christ's commission to make disciples. As with most congregational activities during the quarantines, it may have seemed that the venues for deploying these gifts had disappeared. The usual ways of leading, serving, administrating, teaching, and making use of these gifts were no longer available in person. A congregation needs to help its members understand that while the settings and situations for using these gifts may have shifted, the gifts are still there, and the call of Christ to use them to bless others remains.

The first step in this would be to make certain that the members of the congregation understood what their gifts are. The best way to do this would be to teach about the gifts in the congregation using the digital means available for this. The digital platform could even be leveraged to provide interactive elements, such as a simple spiritual gift assessment quiz that congregation members could take online. This could be built online by the congregation to complement the teaching. An example of an online quiz I developed specifically to aid teaching about different styles of evangelism based on Alan Hirsch and Tim Catchim's discussion of the gift of evangelism can be accessed here: https://markteasdale.net/index.php/quiz/whats-your-evangelism-style/.

Having helped its members discern their gifts, the congregation can then provide new ideas for how these gifts can be used. For some, this will include getting back to in-person engagement to help with essential human needs. As we have seen, even in the most stringent of lockdowns, people still needed to eat and use toilet paper! Those with a gift of serving or hospitality can reach out through pantries or deliveries. As mentioned above, we also saw the mental and emotional toll that isolation had on people. Those with the gift of encouragement can send cards or make calls to let others know they are not alone, and that someone remembers and cares for them. These kinds of personal activities cannot and should not be ignored just because digital activities consume so much of our lives.

For others, it may mean expanding their digital footprint. Those who are called to preach and teach might find themselves more involved with blogging, social media, or videos. Consider the growth of evangelism on the TikTok platform. As one example, York Moore, President and CEO of the Coalition for Christian Outreach, started a new TikTok channel in July 2021 (even though he was already on Facebook, Twitter, and Instagram). By December 2021, he had 143,000 followers and 1.7 million likes on his messages that lay out a very plain call to repent in preparation for God's judgment. Dr. James Foster, a church planter from the AME denomination in Evanston, IL with whom I have had the opportunity to work, had 125,000 followers in December with posts that included singing, brief snippets of sermons, and inspirational and motivational messages meant to help especially young Black men who are struggling. Several additional examples of ways to evangelize specifically through social media are presented by Trisney Bocala-Wiedemann based on input she received from 375 students, ages 15 to 24. The students were responding to a survey that sought to "identify how Adventists can utilize social media platforms to engage more effectively with their audiences in order to build stronger digital spiritual communities that attract youth to the gospel" (Bocala-Wiedemann, 2022).

Many Christians may simply be unaware that the gifts with which the Holy Spirit has empowered them are still viable and actionable during the pandemic and in digital settings. By creating opportunities to rediscover those gifts and to deploy them either physically or digitally, the congregation can launch Christians to provide a welcome and needed witness in the world. And, by grounding this witness in the work of the Holy Spirit within each Christian's life, engaging in this witness will further form Christians as disciples of Jesus Christ.

More importantly, this witness and formation need not come to an end during lockdowns. The same creativity that allows Christians to determine the needs people have and the ways that they can meet those needs by deploying their gifts can continue. Even if the need for toilet paper slows because it is much more plentiful, new needs will arise (like for baby formula). Even if TikTok wanes as the preferred social media platform, a new one will take its place. The important thing is to increase the capacity of Christians to love their neighbors by using their unique gifts. This invites both the Christian and those to whom they minister more fully into the life of Christ.

Congregational Metrics

Finally, how can the congregation keep itself accountable for forming its members and launching them for evangelistic mission?

The best way the congregation can do this is to change its metrics. The old adage is true, "what gets measured gets done." By measuring something, we demonstrate that we value it because we are creating a record through which we can hold ourselves accountable for operating in accordance with our values.

There are plenty of ideas for new church metrics that move beyond counting members, attenders, and dollars. In his book, Wilhoit offered several questions congregational leaders could use to consider whether they were forming people to receive, remember, respond, and relate (Wilhoit, 2008). In my book, *Participating in Abundant Life*, I have an appendix that includes three score cards that congregations can use to track whether their ministries are prompting their members to receive and share the abundant life of Christ, both inside and outside of the church (Teasdale, 2022). They do this by looking at how the church is using its resources, including the activities in which its leaders are most engaged, where it is spending its money, how it is using its facilities, and what partnerships it is forming with other organizations. Regardless of the exact form these new metrics take, the important thing is that they are created and deployed.

To make these metrics more effective, they should not only track congregational activities but also how individual members of a congregation are growing in holiness and engaging in missional activities. One way to do this is to link the data collected and shared in the lifelogs of individual members to the metrics used to determine whether a congregation is being effective in its work to form Christians in holiness and to evangelize those who are not yet Christians. Even if there are no lifelogs being kept, the congregation could provide scorecards their members could use to record how they are using their time, money, energy, and decision-making to seek after holiness and be missionally active (see Teasdale, 2022 for an example).

Ideally, the data from the individual member's scorecards would be aggregated, offering the congregation a way to assess not only how intentionally it is creating opportunities for members to be formed and launched, but to assess the impact that its members are having as the church scattered in the world. The congregation could then be encouraged with stories of how they are collectively growing as an evangelistic witness to the larger community, demonstrating the holy lives into which they are being formed.

A congregation could use a website or app to provide a platform where members fill out this information. Much like journaling or even like Ignatius of Loyola's Prayer of Examen, Christians could move through the online scorecard at the end of each day or week to reflect on how they had lived out their faith. Over many weeks and months, Christians could chart their progress, seeing how they had been formed and where they had engaged in evangelistic practices. This data could be optionally sent to a central congregational hub or to a small group for assessment, accountability, and storytelling. Indeed, there are already some tools like this, harnessing the digital to help track missional activities of their members and creating statistics from this for the congregation as a whole, taking in both physical and digital activities. One example is the "Bless Every Home" app available in the Apple App Store. This app allows users to create accounts and track their progress in evangelizing all the people within a two-mile radius of their homes. Pastors can register their congregations with this app so that the individual evangelistic efforts of the members can be collected to provide an overall picture of the evangelistic work of the congregation.

Conclusion

My youth pastor meant well. He loved us and worked hard on our behalf. Indeed, he was the one who planted the idea for me to enter the ordained ministry. I am deeply grateful for his ministry in my life. At the same time, his understanding of evangelism was stunted and that led to an overall stunting of how he sought to form us as Christians. As he saw it, the church's primary role was that of a gatekeeper who carefully guarded and passed down the truths of the faith, only allowing those who could demonstrate an equal level of care for those truths to join its ranks. It wanted to welcome people to know the truth, but it was wary of letting them too far in prior to vetting them.

Both the biblical witness and current evangelism scholarship argue for a much more holistic understanding of evangelism that requires us not just to know the truth, but to care about the formation of the evangelists. Not only must we be authentic, but we must authentically be seeking after holiness so that the message we proclaim will be credible.

The fact that our lives now entail a digital presence provides Christians a greater opportunity to demonstrate this holy life. The church must step forward to help Christians find new formation practices so they can take hold of this opportunity. They can do this by providing the support and accountability for Christians to have their personal stories interweave with the Christian story through lifelogging, by offering rituals that anchor people in holiness by giving them a way to recognize holy space and time so they are not lost in the time warp of digital activity, and by reminding people of their gifts and helping them find new opportunities to serve others with those gifts. The congregations can further add to this witness and sustain their corporate holiness by adopting new metrics that measure its use of resources to promote this formation and mission.

This is not the first time that the church has been called upon to evangelize and disciple people on the frontier. Moving onto a frontier is admittedly disorienting and requires changes, but the promise of Scripture is that we follow an unchanging God whose call to make disciples remains constant in all contexts. By seeking to be formed in the holiness Christ makes available for us, we will be well prepared to enter this new digital frontier boldly to form saints for Christ and his Kingdom.

References

Abraham, W. J. (1989). *The logic of evangelism*. Eerdmans.

Beck, M. A. & Picardo, R. (2021). *Fresh Expressions in a digital age: How the church can prepare for a post-pandemic world*. Abingdon Press.

Bocala-Wiedemann, T. (2022). Social media as a tool for evangelism. *Great Commission Research Journal, 14*(1), 19-34. https://place.asburyseminary.edu/gcrj/vol14/iss1/2/

Dotzman, A. (2020, October 23). "Digital citizenship and equipping future saints. *Catechist*. https://www.catechist.com/digital-citizenship-equipping-future-saints/.

Estes, D. (2009). *SimChurch: Being the church in the virtual world*. Zondervan.

Gregory, J. B. & Levy, P. E. (2015). *Using feedback in organizational consulting*. American Psychological Association. http://dx.doi.org/10.1037/14619-008.

MacDonald, A., Stetzer, E., Wilson, T., & Yang, D. (2020, April 21) *How church leaders are responding to the challenges of Covid-19: Second round survey*. The Billy Graham Center's Send Institute, Exponential, Leadership Network, Discipleship.org, and ARC. https://multiplication.org/product/covid-report-2/.

Meadows, P. (2012). Mission and discipleship in a digital culture. *Mission Studies, 29*, 163-182.

Reisman, K. (2019). Proclamation. In Michael J. Gehring, Andrew D. Kinsey, and Vaughn W. Baker (Eds.), *The Logic of evangelism revisited* (25-34). Wipf and Stock.

Richardson, R. (2006). *Reimagining evangelism*. IVP.

Robert, D. L. (2022). Dana Robert responds to Mark Teasdale "Extending the metaphor: Evangelism as the heart of mission twenty-five years later". *Methodist Review, 14*, 68–77.

Seversen, B. (2020). *Not done yet: Reaching and keeping unchurched emerging adults*. IVP.

Smith, G. T. (2014). *Called to be saints*. IVP.

Taylor, L. M. (2021). Reaching out online: Learning from one church's embrace of digital worship, ministry and witness. Witness: *The Journal of the Academy for Evangelism in Theological Education, 35,* 1-14.

Teasdale, M. R. (2014). *Methodist evangelism, American salvation.* Cascade.

Teasdale, M. R. (2022). *Participating in abundant life: Holistic salvation for a secular age.* IVP.

Wesley, J. & Wesley C. (1739). *Hymns and sacred poems.* Strahan.

Wilhoit, J. (2008). *Spiritual formation as if the church mattered.* Baker.

About the Author

Mark R. Teasdale is the E. Stanley Jones Professor of Evangelism at Garrett-Evangelical Theological Seminary. His most recent book is *Participating in Abundant Life: Holistic Salvation for a Secular Age* (IVP, 2022). https://markteasdale.net/

GREAT COMMISSION
RESEARCH JOURNAL
2022, Vol. 14(2) 85-102

Apologetics and Disability: Reframing Our Response to the Question of Suffering

Rochelle Scheuermann
Wheaton College

Abstract

A prominent question that is asked when people consider God is how to account for suffering if God is good and all-powerful. For Christians, answering this question is a major part of apologetic and evangelistic training. But what if the way we have traditionally approached this question is not good news for everyone? This paper examines the suffering question in light of disabilities and suggests a new way to engage in apologetics that is centered in creation (not fall) and celebrates the gifts and opportunities that come through a diversity of ability.

The author would like to thank Nathan Mann for his research assistance and thoughts as she gathered background information for this paper.

Introduction

Apologetics is an important partner to evangelism. Alistair McGrath (2012, pp. 21-22) argues that apologetics is distinct from evangelism because it removes obstacles to and establishes a plausibility for Christian faith which evangelism then invites people to embrace. The distinction, he says, is between *consent* and *commitment*, between *conversation* and *invitation* (2012, p. 22). While the purposes and the aims of each are both distinct and alike (to the point that McGrath (2022, p. 22) admits the difference between them is both real and "fuzzy"), one of the greatest commonalities between apologetics and evangelism is the biblical theology undergirding their very frameworks. Clearing the ground of obstacles and inviting people to a new way of life both rely on core theological convictions about God, the world, and his mission to redeem it. Central to both, then, is a biblical narrative that spans creation, fall, redemption, and new creation. Though I will expound on this in more nuanced detail later, for many evangelicals, this narrative includes the following main points: The world God created was perfect. Human beings messed it up. Jesus' death and resurrection resolved what we could not. Someday the fullness of God's kingdom will come and humans in fully perfected bodies will enjoy a fully perfected new heaven and earth. Where evangelism invites people to participate in this grand story, apologetics uses this story to address specific questions and concerns that often prevent people from considering or maintaining Christian faith.

As an evangelical, I embrace this storyline of creation, fall, redemption, and new creation. It is a theological foundation for faith and witness, and I believe accurately captures God's mission and work. However, I do wonder if we have limited (and even distorted) the expanse of God's story by how we tell it and, in so doing, have created more obstacles to faith for some rather than removing them. To set the stage for the rest of this paper and the main question I want to address, let me share a personal story.

Until I became a mom, I did not really question the basic Christian narrative I inherited. The world was perfect. We messed it up. Through Jesus, God is in the process of fixing it. This narrative served me well until the night I encountered a well-meaning lady from a church. She and I shared a Pentecostal background, and she was coming to me with a strong reservoir of healing faith. However, her question to me was startling. She began the conversation by mentioning how she was recently in a prayer meeting where they prayed for God to heal a child with autism and she was struck by a thought which she voiced to me, "If God healed *your* son, do you think God would also change your son's physical features?" She asked her question both with innocence and eager faith and yet, I found myself at a loss for words. My head was shouting back, "Healed? From what does my son need to be healed?" My son was born with Down syndrome. The presence of an extra chromosome affects the speed of his cognitive and physical development. And this extra chromosome is also very much central to his identity, personality, and being. There is nothing I would change about him because to have a "normal" number of chromosomes would be to erase the boy that God created and that I love. I would never want that. Ever. And yet her question haunted me.

When I began teaching my next apologetics class, I found my lens changed. A key question within apologetics is making sense of suffering and evil. By the end of the course, student after student gave the same theological response to this apologetic question.

> *When God created the world, it was perfect. But when we chose to disobey God, we brought sin into the world which has affected every aspect of the world. Because of our sin, it means that people now do bad things to one another. It means that creation is distorted. It means that sickness and disease and natural disasters came into the world. But this is not how God created us or our world. And the good news is that God came into the world as Jesus and died on the Cross for us. By rising from the dead, he is able to destroy sin and he promises that he is now in the process of creating a new heaven and earth. And when we put our faith in him, one day we will live with him forever. And he promises that in heaven, there will be no sin, no suffering, no sickness, and no death.*

Told this way, the narrative is hopeful for those ravaged by cancer or victims of assault or natural disaster. This world is not what God intended. All the suffering we see is because of sin. Someday, it will all be taken care of and made right. But what about for people like my son? As I graded papers and saw this single narrative repeated over and over in such concrete terms, I did not find this a fully good-news story. As an adoptive mom, I went into motherhood with my eyes open: I freely chose the disability from the beginning. Even so, this has not lessened all of the burdens or challenges of raising a special needs child and it certainly has not lessened the questions I ask and am asked about disability. Is it true that the only reason my son was born with an extra chromosome was because Adam and Eve ate the fruit? How do I reconcile this with the notion that God formed us in the womb (Ps 139:13-18)? If my son's extra chromosome is a result of sin coming into the world and distorting creation, does this mean new creation requires that extra chromosome be eliminated? Does this mean that the very things that make him *him* are the very things that God will reject in new creation? If not, then why do we keep telling the story as if all disability is a result of sin and must be remedied in heaven?

As I sit with these questions and as I sit with parents asking for the first or the hundredth time why their child has this or that disability, I cannot help but wonder if our apologetic and evangelistic approaches are based on a biblical narrative that is read solely from an abled perspective. How might a disability perspective refine the ways in which we understand and tell this story? While this question can take us in a myriad of directions and cause us to dive deeply into topics long debated by theologians, I focus this paper specifically on how apologists frame the conversation. To that end, this paper will outline how various apologists answer the question of suffering, overlay these answers with disability perspectives, and then suggest a reframed way of discussing suffering in apologetic and evangelistic encounters.

Accounting for Suffering and Evil if God is Good

Apologists note that one of the most prevalent questions asked by seekers and skeptics is how to make sense of suffering in the world. Even for the Christian, the idea of suffering is problematic (Keller, 2008, p. 27). For some people, the question is existential. If God really existed there would not be suffering and evil in the world in the first place. For others, it is experiential. They have personally encountered suffering in a particular way and cannot reconcile it with a good God (i.e., if God is all-powerful but does not prevent suffering, he is not good; if God is good but cannot prevent suffering, he is not all-powerful). Knowing which concern people are raising requires apologists to ask clarifying questions and to listen well. Even so, both trajectories ultimately lead apologists to address some key issues. (1) How do we account for suffering and evil in the world? (2) Why does God allow suffering and evil? (3) Does suffering have meaning or is it pointless?

In *The Reason for God*, Tim Keller (2008, pp. 223-236) describes the four-part drama of the Bible (creation, fall, redemption, and restoration) as a dance. God found such joy in "mutually self-giving love" (p. 224) that he created human beings in order to share it (p. 228). We were invited into a dance in which God was central. However, we lost the dance when we changed from orbiting our lives around God to "trying to get God to orbit around us" (229). Our self-centeredness disintegrated everything, leading to individual, social, and cosmic consequences (pp. 170-177). Keller (p. 177) argues that because

> Human beings are so integral to the fabric of things...when human beings turned from God the entire warp and woof of the world unraveled. Disease, genetic disorders, famine, natural disasters, aging, and death itself are as much the result of sin as are oppression, war,

crime, and violence. We have lost God's shalom--physically, spiritually, socially, psychologically, culturally. Things now fall apart. In Romans 8, Paul says that the entire world is now 'in bondage to decay' and 'subject to futility' and will not be put right until we are put right.

Joshua Chatraw and Mark Allen (2018) similarly note that God "created the universe to be good" (p. 54) with human beings playing an essential role within creation. As "God's image bearers," our duty was "to rule over the earth...to represent him on earth by stewarding his creation and, in some sense, extending his rule over it" (p. 45). Our disobedience, however, has distorted God's good creation and introduced "human suffering, pain, and evil," things we know "are wrong" and not as God intended (p. 54). "Evil," therefore, "is anything that stands against God and his plan for creation (p. 274).

Gregory Boyd, in *Is God to Blame?* (2003), latches onto this idea that evil opposes God and his plan for creation by arguing that the world is in the state of spiritual conflict. Though Adam and Eve exercised their free will and disobeyed, Satan, too, exercised his free will and now rules the present world, seeking to disrupt and destruct God's creative purposes. The suffering we face can be attributed to this Satanic war against God.

While sharing the sentiment that the world, once "unstained by sin or suffering or death" (McLaughlin, 2019, 205) is now fallen and not as God intended, Alister McGrath (2012) and Rebecca McLaughlin (2019) add additional nuances to the discussion. For McLaughlin (2019, p. 203), "sin and suffering are clearly connected in a universal sense;" however, we should not equate suffering with (punishment for) sin. "The amount of suffering a person endures," she says, "is not proportional to his or her sin" (p. 203). For McGrath (2012, p. 165-166), human actions of selfishness have brought significant consequences to our personal, social, and cosmic existence. However, not every natural event is the result of Adam and Eve's sin. Sometimes "suffering arises from the way this world is" and McGrath (2012, p. 166) argues, "We have no reason to believe there could be a 'better' world." Tectonic plates, for example, are necessary for life on earth. While the result of such shifting plates can be earthquakes and tsunamis, these are not "*evil*...they're just *natural*" (p. 165). Though these are not intended to cause suffering, they do, and this is just "part of the price we pay for living in a world in which life is possible" (p. 165).

In accounting for evil and suffering in the world, all of our apologists see the world God created as good and blame sin for changing the world into something God did not intend. Though McGrath leaves open the possibility that the natural working of the world could have produced suffering prior to the fall, he and the others all attribute disorder, discord, disease, and death to our disobedience. God created a good world, but we messed it up. Boyd alone emphasizes the enormous role that Satan has in continued suffering and evil.

If we conclude that a good God exists and that he created a good world, why is it that God permits evil and suffering to continue? After all, "the loving, omnipotent God of our imagination would move swiftly from creation to new creation, from the Garden of Eden of Genesis to the heavenly Jerusalem of Revelation" (McLaughlin, 2019, p. 204). Why didn't he? Paul Gould (2019) proposes two trajectories of inquiry. One trajectory suggests that "God has a morally justified reason for evil" that we do not always know (Gould, 2019, 188). Just because we cannot find a reason for suffering does not mean that there is not one (Keller 2008, p. 23). Though "we can't plumb the depths on the meaning of suffering," Keller (2008, pp. 24-25) says that many attest to how it brought good into their lives. In the midst of the suffering, we cannot see clearly, but "with time and perspective most of us can see good reasons for at least some of the tragedy and pain that occurs in life" (Keller 2008, p. 25). If we can see the good for some suffering, is it not possible that God might see good for all of it (Keller 2008, 2 p. 5, cf. Gould, 2019, p. 188)? McGrath (2012, p. 163) agrees, finding the atheistic argument of Richard Dawkins, that "suffering is pointless and meaningless—and is exactly what we should expect in a universe that itself has no purpose" to be "deeply [dissatisfying]."

This leads us to the second trajectory of inquiry: can we discern some of those reasons why God allows suffering? For many theologians and apologists, theodicies provide us with a way forward. The most popular theodicies include "the free will theodicy (God wants us to be self-determiners of our character and actions, and when we misuse our free will, evil results), the soul-making theodicy (God uses pain and suffering to grow our character), and the greater-goods theodicy (God brings about greater goods as a result of evil)" (Gould, 2019, p. 188). This resonates with Chatraw and Allen (2018, p. 53) who argue that suffering has a variety of reasons ranging from negative to positive: a result of our own sin and disobedience, due to others' sin, for greater divine good, for insight into God, because of obedience, for sharing in Christ's suffering, as a means of discipline, for spiritual growth, and to prove faith.

McLaughlin (2019, p. 206) nuances this question in a way that suggests suffering has a more integral role in bringing us to "earth-shattering intimacy with God." Though God did not will Adam and Eve to sin, neither did he draw a "much shorter, straighter line…between the beginning and the end" (p. 206). We may not be able to understand why

God allowed suffering, but only with suffering can we "truly bond" and know Jesus "far more intimately: as Savior, Lover, Husband, Head, Brother, Fellow Sufferer, and [our] Resurrection and [our] Life" (p. 206). McLaughlin (206) believes that to say, "humanity was very good," was to also say, "it was not the best. The best, from a biblical perspective, was yet to come. And the way to get there would be through suffering." The ultimate promise, she says, is for every tear to be wiped away and death to be no more (Rev 21:4), not that "God will not allow us to cry in the first place. What end could possibly be worth all this pain? Jesus says he is" (p. 206).

Though Gould, Keller, McGrath, Chatraw and Allen, and McLaughlin argue that our own sin brought suffering and evil into the world, none suggest that we have been left to wallow in our consequences. Our own finitude prevents us from knowing all the reasons why God allows suffering to continue; however, it does not mean there are not reasons. But even where this may not give us comfort, we can find assurance in God's understanding (he suffered for us), God's care (he can bring good out of the most impossible situations), God's justice (he will judge sin), and God's rescuing power (he is making and will ultimately make all things right).

It is here that Boyd's perspective stands out. Boyd challenges the notion that God somehow wills or allows evil to persist. To suggest that God has morally justified reasons for evil and suffering (Gould's first trajectory) is tantamount to saying God wills evil. And to say God wills evil is to attribute evil to God, which contradicts everything Scripture tells us about God's nature. Boyd argues, instead, that the evil and suffering we see in the world is a direct result of spiritual conflict, between God's good creative purposes and Satan's attempts to challenge them. In Jesus, the Kingdom of God is coming on Earth as it is in Heaven, and one day Jesus's reign will be fully established for all eternity. Until that day, Boyd recognizes a lot of ambiguity and mystery related to God's providence and sovereignty seen alongside the destructive purposes of Satan. While Boyd's perspective shifts somewhat from that of our other apologists, he ends up taking the conversation further in terms of disability. Keller directly attributes disability (disease, genetic disorders, etc.) to sin and Gould, McGrath, Chatraw and Allen, and McLaughlin indirectly do so as well. We choose to sin and the entrance of it somehow broke the perfectly working systems in the world including nature. Boyd suggests that because Satan tampers with God's good plan, God has no part in disabilities. God does not will "which *individuals* will be born mute or deaf. He simply asserts that he is Creator of the kind of world in which some people become disabled" (Boyd, 2003, p. 188). For Boyd (188), Scripture is "clear...infirmities such as muteness or blindness originate from Satan" and God's role is "to empower human mediators to free people from these afflictions." All of our apologists come to the same endpoint: new creation will end affliction. For those (particularly Boyd and Keller) that equate disability with affliction, new creation will necessarily end disability as well. To understand why this may not ring as "good news" for all people, we turn now to a brief look at what we mean by disability and how disability perspectives might challenge our beliefs about suffering.

Understanding Disability and Disability Perspectives

It is challenging to define disability in one sense because the concept covers a range of issues that can be temporary or permanent, inherited or acquired, and affect a person physically or mentally. Where people fall on this spectrum often affects their outlook and the kinds of questions they ponder. To navigate through these complexities, we will consider three models of disability.

The *medical model* locates disability within individual bodies and defines disability as any deviation from the assumed norms of how we think a body or mind should work. This model emphasizes people's limitations and often reduces people to the function of their disabilities (Reynolds 2008, p. 25). Since it is "assumed that disability indicates a deficient or flawed human condition...which holds a person back from participating in society," disability necessarily needs to be treated, "fixed, made better, or overcome" (Reynolds 2008, p. 25). For this reason, the "principle of normalization" exists at its core, "attempting to modify, repair, or relocate individuals with disabilities until they are congruent with societal expectations of normalcy and acceptability" (Creamer 2009, p. 24).

The *social model* of disability moves the focus to the socially constructed environments and attitudes that bar people from full participation. Where the medical model assumes that people with key functional deviations (e.g., deaf, paraplegic, developmental delays) *are* disabled, the social model says people *become* disabled "insofar as they experience prejudice and exclusion" (Creamer 2009, p. 25). Individual diagnoses are no longer problematized; rather, physical spaces, social attitudes, systems, and points of access are brought under the microscope.

The *cultural model* of disability embraces and celebrates disability as a marker of group identity and a contribution to human diversity (Berger 2013, p. 29). Within this model, socially constructed ideas of normalcy are challenged by the belief that disability is simply one way "of being embodied in the world" (Berger 2013, p. 29). The cultural model critiques the medical model's assumption that bodies need to be fixed. The cultural model also critiques some aspects of social models for "still presuming a 'normal' way of being embodied ... [that] emphasize the sameness, rather than the diversity of bodies" (Bennett and Volpe 2018, p. 123). Cultural and social location matter for disability and the cultural model not only suggests that disability is an "intertwinement of modes of thought depending on particular situations and circumstances" but also highlights "the potential of disability as a state of being" (Devlieger 2005, p. 8).

To navigate the space between these models, defining terms becomes paramount. *Impairment* highlights the biological/physiological loss. *Disability* explains when an impairment disables one from performing certain tasks due to physical and social barriers (cf. Yong 2011, pp. 8-12; Creamer 2009, p. 27; Berger 2013, p. 6). Though these definitions suggest distinct boundaries of experience, reality reveals the complication that many with disabilities embody because they can experience a range of difficulties in tandem with, apart from, or solely due to social limitations.

This brief overview of disability is very instructive to our question of how apologists answer the suffering question. First, it becomes easy to see that many people in the church embrace a medical model of disability. It is clear from Keller and Boyd, in particular, that disability is located within individual bodies that are judged to be broken (whether due to disease, genetics, or accident). With such clear evidence of sin being manifest in biological and physiological ways, it is not surprising that they and the other apologists we have examined, embrace "the modern Christian expectation that Jesus's healing is simply about curing malfunctions in individuals' bodies" (Brock, 2021, p. 26). Though theologian Brian Brock explicitly says this "is a truncated gospel" (p. 26), Christians often assume Jesus healed every person he met and, thus, a healed, whole body is desirable and best (p. 45). Boyd (2003, p. 187) is most explicit on this point arguing that "Jesus and the Gospel authors uniformly diagnosed muteness, deafness, blindness, and other infirmities as directly or indirectly coming from the devil...Jesus demonstrated God's will for people by removing these infirmities." Such an abled reading overlooks how Jesus heals (neither intrusively nor forcefully), when or if Jesus heals, and the many ways in which Jesus enacts social and spiritual restoration over physical healing (see Brock, 2021, p. 44, cf. Fox, 2019).

Second, the medical model of disability highlights the ways that apologists uncritically equate disability with suffering and affliction. Because the non-disabled are beholden to normate assumptions (perspectives "presumed to be adequate for measuring the experiences of all people, which then invalidates the points of view of those who don't see or hear similarly, who do things differently, or who simply are different" [Yong, 2011, p. 11]), the non-disabled often "impute suffering" to the disabled (Yong, 2011, p. 12). We often take our own experience as the frame of reference for evaluating the burden of a given disability and, in so doing, can ascribe more pain or suffering to the other person than the actual experience. For example, Boyd (2003, p. 188) unequivocally calls deafness an affliction (from Satan) and in need of God's restoration. Many in the Deaf community would vehemently rebut this, believing that Deaf culture has "particular languages, and important contributions for society" (Bennett and Volpe, 2018, p. 122). The medical model fails to recognize the ways in which "a medical 'good' may result in the loss of other, perhaps less tangible goods" (Bennett and Volpe, 2018, p. 122). In the same way, when our theology is solely informed by a medical model of disability, we often fail to recognize the ways in which a "theological good" (i.e., healing) may result in the loss of other, perhaps less tangible goods (i.e., the needed gifts, perspectives, and corrections that come to us through the disabled experience and the lives of people with disabilities). I must explicitly state here that I do not mean that people with disabilities are here solely to be an object lesson for the non-disabled. I mean, rather, that people with disabilities have their own gifts and perspectives that the body of Christ needs for it to be whole and functional (see Scheuermann, 2022). When our apologetic narratives attribute all disability to sin, Satan, and suffering, it becomes harder to celebrate the many good things that disability adds to the world and the church.

Third, while all of our apologists suggest there have been massive social and cosmic ramifications to Adam and Eve's sin and Satan's continued campaign to disrupt God's good world, by solely understanding disability through the medical model, these apologists do not address the role of social and physical environments in creating and perpetuating disability. For the disabled, these apologists can only offer the hope of healed bodies in the eschaton. What this fails to consider is how ability or disability may not be the real issue. If God's new kingdom does overcome the social and cosmic results of sin (which all of our apologists argue will happen), then many of the prejudicial attitudes and social barriers that turn impairments into disabilities will be eradicated in the eschaton, eliminating the need for everyone to be "healed" by making full space for the flourishing of people with diverse levels of ability.

Finally, the cultural model of disability reveals the ways in which our apologists see disability as something that happens *to* someone and is separate from the core of their identity. For Keller (2008, p. 177), disability is a consequence of sin disrupting the world's natural order. For McGrath (2012, p. 165), some occurrences in nature are just part of being in a living world. For Chatraw and Allen (2018, p. 53), suffering is either a byproduct of sin or the means to a better (i.e., more godly, more satisfied, more glorious) end. For McLaughlin (2019, p. 206) the raw story in the middle between the Bible's happy introduction and conclusion is what makes new creation (with its lack of tears, death, mourning, crying, and pain) worth it. For Boyd (2003, p. 188), God does not will who is afflicted with disability, but does will that all disability be healed. If, indeed, disability is something that happens *to* people, removing or healing the disability makes sense in every circumstance. But for many people with disabilities, the disability is a core part of how they know and experience the world and of how they know and experience themselves. Removing the disability would fundamentally change their identity. People without disabilities are surprised to learn that, when identity is on the line, many disabled, especially those with congenital disabilities, do not want healing.

When we bring disability studies into conversation with apologetics, we are able to consider the certainty we have about the eschaton more circumspectly. We can be confident that in the new heaven and earth there will be "no more death or mourning or crying or pain" (Rev. 21:4) and "nothing impure will ever enter it" (Rev. 21:27). We can be confident that resurrected bodies will be imperishable, immortal, raised in glory and power, and changed (1 Cor 15:42-58). But does this necessitate the "healing" of every aspect of disability?

Those who follow the elimination theory would say yes. This theory works from the premise that because sin marred the perfection of God's creation, heaven is the great reversal where God will restore all things to "what they were meant to be" (Gould, 2016, p. 317). J.B. Gould (2016, p. 318) argues passionately for this view, suggesting that when people cannot function according to "a design that is typical of their species," their disability inhibits "normal abilities [which] enable people to perform major life activities—and thereby to experience the important aspects of flourishing God created us for." Among the requirements for flourishing, according to Gould (2017, p. 100), are "a bundle of goods such as personal relationships, productive activity (career and leisure pursuits), and individual autonomy." Believing that "intellectual competence is a precondition of relational life," and that "human beings are teleological beings made for the supernatural end of love and union with God," Gould (2016, p. 330) argues that without healing, people with cognitive disabilities would be unable to experience eternal joy. Eliminationists, then, thread the needle between creation and fall by suggesting that disability "does not exclude the person being *imago Dei* or impair one's human dignity" but rather is "a privation of what naturally 'should' be present" (Ehrman, 2015, p. 732). While the disabled are good creations who can contribute meaningfully to the world, they experience deficiencies and limitations that "are contrary to God's will and plan" (Gould, 2016, p. 321). For this reason, Gould posits that in heaven "if disability is not healed, then evil is not finally eliminated" (p. 324). But as evil has been conquered through Jesus, the elimination view assumes that "disability is not retained in any capacity in the future kingdom" (Gosbell, 2021, p. 6). Jennifer Anne Cox (2017, p. 48) points to the scars of the resurrected Jesus as proof that disability is healed and, thus, "those who believe in Jesus will not experience disability in their resurrected state either."

Those who follow the retention view would argue that some aspects of disability will be present in the eschaton, especially when "some impairments are so identity-constitutive that their removal would involve the obliteration of the person as well" (Yong, 2011, p. 121). Retentionists agree that there will be transformation of bodies in the resurrection but disagree that this necessarily *requires* bodies to "be free of the marks of our present impairments" (2011, p. 122) or without "continuity between the present and the future body" (p. 123). Of equal concern for retentionists is how heaven transforms "the world's scale of values as a whole" (p. 122). Where eliminationists believe disability prevents human flourishing (defined as productivity, relationality, and possessing self-determination—see Gould, 2016 and 2017), retentionists argue that the preservation of Jesus' scars in his resurrected body challenge "conceptions about the nature of bodily perfection" (Gosbell, 2021, p. 4, cf. Eiesland 1994) and "our underlying assumptions about what it means to be human and what human flourishing entails" (Whitaker, 2019a, p. 4). Yong (2011, p. 135) argues that redeemed, rather than eliminated, disabilities are the means through which "divine power, wisdom, and glory are...most clearly and finally magnified," a "'transvaluation' of disability in the resurrection body [that] is not unique to Jesus' resurrection" (Gosbell, 2021, p. 3). Whitaker (2019b) clarifies that only the person with a disability can truly determine how defining impairments are to his or her identity and wonders whether "some persons may retain their disabilities" while "others might not." She is confident, however, that "in the case of our own resurrection, we will not be in doubt as to our identity or existence when the time comes."

The elimination and retention views present seemingly opposed proposals that attempt to make sense of disability. Yet both are shaped by modernity and its elevation of the individual person (Gosbell, 2021, p. 8). Perhaps this is where our contemporary apologetic perspectives also fall short. We tell the cosmic story of God in a way that can easily put the individual person in the center. And when we do, we cannot help but see disability as a travesty for individual people. It is here that Brian Brock (2019) challenges us to reconsider our theological center and through his proposal, provides us a pathway for a new apologetic approach as well.

Brock (2019) argues that the ways we usually talk about disability are anthropocentric and centered in the fall. This is clearly seen in our apologists who foreground the body as the locus of disability and ground their entire suffering apologetic in the fall. Regardless of whether the apologist then moves toward a retentionist or eliminationist view, this leads apologists toward "an anthropologically oriented definition of healing and redemption" that reads "the resurrected body through a view of the created body" (p. 182). By positioning human identity within the individual body, Brock says we fail to take seriously the "epistemic and ecclesial implications of eschatology" which center on the reminder that "human redemption is into a redeemed *community*" (2019, p. 183). For Brock, this shifts the focus from future speculation about the state of individually resurrected bodies to the present, starting our eschatological understanding from the same place that the New Testament begins, "the new social order that is *already* being established" (p. 184). The New Testament is not generally concerned with the resurrected state of individuals, offering few hints about what healing looks like in the eschaton. Rather, New Testament eschatology "[resituates] our sensate relation to God, world, and the neighbor" by fostering "*an embodied expectation that Jesus' heavenly kingdom of peace will arrive here and now*" (p. 185). Ultimately, "anthropologically ordered eschatological speculations are...not a solution to the pains of this life" (p. 192). Focusing so intently on perfection of bodies in creation and new creation leaves the present unaddressed and, in this sense, unredeemed. A holistic, New Testament eschatology foregrounds the interconnectedness of people with God and each other, which consequently backgrounds bodies. Brock (p. 192) says,

> Put in technical terms, an eschatology oriented by notions of past and future or by a strong interest in anthropological definition is less illuminative of the theologically crucial aspects of life together than an eschatology oriented by conceptions of sociality, vocation, and the real and effected transformation of perception.

In the *redeemed* community, people with disabilities participate in the edification of the church (and by extension the world). And in the *redeemed* community, life in the local church "challenges the individualized and medicalized account of [the lives of people with disability] that assumes [their] most important need is for therapies that will solve [their] (individual) problems and deficiencies" (p. 193). This does not negate the reality that sin does break things in the world and Brock acknowledges that disability "does expose the sin of the world" (p. 194). However, he is careful to not locate the sin within the individual body or say that "sin and brokenness of the created order...define [the disabled person's] being and life as a whole" (p. 194). The disabled body is "a *vector* of the divine annunciation of mercy to the world" revealing the myriad of ways that each person is broken (p. 194). It is through eschatological ecclesiology, then, that Brock (p. 194), reflecting on his own son, can

> ...remain agnostic about the causality of Adam's biological condition. I can affirm that his twenty-first chromosome probably would not have become conjoined in an unfallen world. But I can also affirm that the fact that every cell of his body has been impacted by this biological "fault" says very little about who he has been created to be. I can affirm both that he will be redeemed from pain in the resurrection, and that God has given him to his family, his church, and his nation just as he is. There is no other, better, or different Adam who was not affected by his genetic palette. Having been given him by God establishes my vocation as parent, engaging me in an extended work of responsibility and receipt. I have been presented with a limit I can love. With it comes divine confrontation and judgement of my habits as well as the habits of the world that live in me.

Gosbell (2021, p. 9) reminds us that since the fall "corrupted every aspect of human existence" this includes our ability "to measure the value of ourselves and others, to recognize true identity, to embrace diversity, [and] to understand limitations." We see through a glass darkly (1 Cor 13:12) and, thus, cannot ultimately know what the future looks like. However, we live in the present, and it is here that we are called to attend. Calling Paul's 1 Cor 12 Body of Christ metaphor a "blueprint for how believers are to live today," Gosbell (2021, p. 11) urges us to value and accept "all members of the Body, not for who they might become in the future kingdom, but for who they are now as valuable and contributing members of Christ's body." We are not autonomous or independent creatures, but rather "wholly dependent on God and designed to live in community as both providers and recipients of each other's gifts" (Gosbell, 2021, p. 11). And it is this communal vision that gives us a new apologetic.

A New Apologetic

One of the problems with our apologetic starting point is the assumption that, with regard to disabilities, "the real questions are about the *origins* of disabling conditions" (Brock 2021, p. 96). Much more salient to people with disabilities and their families is less a matter of *cause* and more a concern with discovering "a theological account of the *goodness* of people's lives *as they are*" (96). Such a shift does not diminish the role of sin in the world—sin really does mess things up—rather it keeps it in its place by not allowing it to undermine the "'it was good' of God's decree over what God has created" (p. 106). A "Christian account of creation, sin, and disability" acknowledges (1) that the limitations and bodily forms God made us with are good, (2) that sin can damage bodies in irreparable ways, and (3) that everyone's body will eventually present problems (106). A Christian account of creation also acknowledges that every human is created in the image of God (Gen 1:26-27), with the ability to "image Christ to one another" through "life-giving relationships across difference." Such "bodily difference and uniqueness" become "part of each person's vocation" (p. 109) and service within community.

Human beings were not created "to be *simply* bodies" but rather intricately interwoven with God and each other in loving relationships (Brock 2019, p. 159). Humans were created with boundaries and limitations (p. 157), and they experience shalom when they learn "to live as creatures...[taking] their satisfaction from God and not from their material surroundings" (p. 154). "To confess the Christian God as Creator," Brock subsequently argues, means "concretely, to be liberated not to *transcend* creation, [the sin of Adam and Eve] but to *receive one's true being in Christ*...by learning what it means to be a creature, that is, to recognize and freely embrace loving relations with other persons as and where they are, with all their brokenness and angularity" (p. 160). Since "human beings were created to be conformed to Christ, and to be resurrected in this conformity to Christ," new creation is less about retaining an "ideal self" and more about retaining those marks that "indicate the role of [a] particular person in their own place, time, and body in God's redemptive story with the world" (p. 184).

This affirmation that *everyone* is a good creation and that *everyone* has a vocational calling dependent on their bodily differences, limitations, and giftings opens "a door to another world" (McGrath 2012, p. 22) for those struggling to understand disability as it relates to themselves and others. A truly Christian account of disability incorporates difference into the church as a "communal treasure" (Brock, 2019, p. 193) and honors the roles that people with disabilities "play in God's own story of his people, as commemorated by and enacted in the worshipping community" (p. 195). This kind of redeemed community, offered through Christ by the working of the Spirit, challenges and displaces "the politics of liberal democracies, with their rooting in individual autonomy and agnostic struggle to secure one's own interests" (p. 197). Because the Gospel story is more of a communal story than an individual one, it is able to make place for interdependence and difference in ways that the world cannot.

By shifting our apologetic response to suffering and disability from an anthropologically centered view of the fall to an ecclesiological and eschatological view of creation, we move from tragedy to opportunity, from limitation as individual loss to limitation as gifts of difference within community. By reframing our eschatological hope from the future healing of broken bodies to the present inbreaking of a new community wherein the Spirit enables everyone to give and receive gifts, we offer a place in the now for people with disabilities and a hope for the future that true suffering will end without the erasing of differences altogether. When we can truly offer the witness of a redeemed community, we can offer people a place where difference is valued and where people "see the beauty in all kinds of people's bodies. Not because they are just looking at bodies but because they have learned to cherish the gifts that God has given through each person" (Brock 2021, p. 132).

For my son, the starting place of understanding his life is not "he exists because sin messed up creation." The starting place is truly "God created his every cell, and this is good." And when this shift is made, the response to his disability changes too. One woman saw my son's disability as a result of sin and assumed he needed healing. However, a different woman at a different church about a year later saw my son's disability through the eyes of ecclesiological eschatology and exclaimed, "I can't wait to see what gifts God has for the church through your son." This is good news.

References

Bennett, J. M., & Volpe, M. A. (2018). Models of disability from religious tradition: Introductory editorial." *Journal of Disability & Religion* 22(2), 121-120. https://www.doi.org/10.1080/23312521.2018.1482134

Berger, R. J. (2013). *Introducing disability studies*. Lynne Rienner Publishers.

Boyd, G. A. (2003). *Is God to blame? Beyond pat answers to the problem of suffering*. IVP Academic.

Brock, B. (2021). *Disability: Living into the diversity of Christ's body*. Baker Academic.

Brock, B. (2019). *Wondrously wounded: Theology, disability, and the body of Christ*. Baylor University Press.

Chatraw, J. D., & Allen, M. (2018). *Apologetics at the cross: An introduction for Christian witness*. Zondervan Academic.

Cox, J. A. (2017). *Jesus the disabled God*. Resource Publications.

Creamer, D. B. (2009). *Disability and Christian theology: Embodied limits and constructive possibilities*. Oxford University Press.

Devlieger, P. J. (2005, October 14-16). *Generating a cultural model of disability* [Conference presentation]. 19th Congress of the European Federation of Associations of Teachers of the Deaf (FEAPDA). https://www.researchgate.net/profile/Patrick-Devlieger/publication/237762101_Generating_a_cultural_model_of_disability/links/5434004f0cf2dc341daf2bc1/Generating-a-cultural-model-of-disability.pdf

Ehrman, T. (2015). Disability and resurrection identity. *New Blackfriars, 96*(1066), 723–738. https://doi.org/10.1111/nbfr.12126

Eiesland, N. L. (1994). *The disabled God: Toward a liberatory theology of disability*. Abingdon Press.

Fox, B. (2019). *Disability and the way of Jesus: Holistic healing in the Gospels and the church*. IVP Academic.

Gosbell, L. A. (2021). Space, place, and the ordering of materiality in disability theology: locating disability in the resurrection and the body of Christ. *Journal of Disability & Religion, 26*(1), 149-161. https://doi.org/10.1080/23312521.2021.1976697

Gould, J. B. (2016). The hope of heavenly healing of disability part 1: Theological issues. *Journal of Disability & Religion, 20*(4), 317-334. https://www.doi.org/10.1080/23312521.2016.1239153

Gould, J.B. (2017). The hope of heavenly healing of disability part 2—Philosophical issues. *Journal of Disability & Religion, 21*(1), 98-116. https://doi.org/10.1080/23312521.2016.1270177

Gould, P. M. (2019). *Cultural apologetics: Renewing the Christian voice, conscience, and imagination in a disenchanted world*. Zondervan.

Keller, T. (2008). *The reason for God: Belief in an age of skepticism*. Penguin Books.

McGrath, A. (2012) *Mere apologetics: How to help seekers and skeptics find faith*. Baker Books.

McLaughlin, R. (2019). *Confronting Christianity: 12 hard questions for the world's largest religion*. Crossway.

Reynolds, T. E. (2008). *Vulnerable communion: A theology of disability and hospitality*. Brazos Press.

Scheuermann, P. (2022) Not whole without us: Including people with disabilities in our understanding of the church, the gospel, and the world." *Missiology: An International Review, 50*(3), 290-303. https://www.doi.org/10.1177/00918296211048832

Whitaker, M. (2019a). The disabled resurrection body and human flourishing: Allowing eschatological possibilities to inform ethics [Paper presentation]. Unpublished Presentation SSCE Annual Conference, London School of Theology.

Whitaker, M. (2019b). Perfected yet still disabled? Continuity of embodied identity in resurrection life. *Stimulus, 26*(2), n.p. https://hail.to/laidlaw-college/article/sRNklJP#_edn20

Yong, A. (2011). *The Bible, disability, and the church: A new vision of the people of God.* Eerdmans.

About the Author

Rochelle Scheuermann (Ph.D., Trinity Evangelical Divinity School) is Associate Professor of Evangelism and Leadership at Wheaton College where she directs three master's degree programs. Her research interests include disability and ministry and preaching and culture.

GREAT COMMISSION
RESEARCH JOURNAL
2022, Vol. 14(2) 103-114

Gerontic Evangelism

Yakubu Jakada
Tri-State Bible College

Abstract

Gerontic Evangelism focuses on sharing the gospel with senior adults. Many evangelism ministries are focusing on children, youth, women, and other adult members of society, but few focus on the elderly. Senior adults in most cases are not seen as a peculiar group that needs to be strategically reached with the gospel. Their importance in society and their growing population worldwide should attract the attention of evangelists and missionaries to target them as a special group for gospel witness. This paper argues that winning the senior adults to Christ is a necessity and may open doors for the evangelization and even the conversion of family members and members of the wider community. This research used participant observation and informal discussions to gather the data for this paper. This paper has the goal of calling the attention of the church and evangelistic organizations to see the need to have a focused evangelistic ministry to senior adults.

Keywords: Gerontic, Gerontology, elderly, evangelism, strategy, senior adults, gospel, witness, ministry

----

Introduction

Senior Adults are very important in society and are precious to God. In some cultures, they are the gatekeepers of their families, clans, tribes, and or communities. There are prospects of open doors for further witness to people who are within the sphere of influence of the seniors who are won to Christ. The growing population of senior adults worldwide calls for the church to pay special attention to evangelizing them. The National Institutes of Health of the United States reported, "The world's older population continues to grow at an unprecedented rate. Today, 8.5 percent of people worldwide (617 million) are aged 65 and over.... This percentage is projected to jump to nearly 17 percent of the world's population by 2050 (1.6 billion)" (Cire, 2016). This report argues for paying special attention to the evangelization of senior adults. It covers a theology of evangelism to establish the biblical basis for evangelism. Some basic information about senior adults helpful for reaching them with the gospel is also covered. The paper discusses strategies for reaching senior adults with the gospel covering the why, the who, and the how of evangelizing them. The goal is to challenge the church, evangelists, and missionaries to focus on this group that is special to God.

Theology of Evangelism

The concept of evangelism can be traced to the Old Testament prophets who were dedicated to calling the nation of Israel to turn from the worship of idols to serve Yahweh (Isaiah 1:18-20; Jeremiah 7:5-7; Amos 4:6). The preaching ministry of Jesus to all the cities and villages is an evangelistic model from the Master Evangelist, Christ himself (Matthew 9:35). He called men to repentance and transformation; he invited people to be part of the Kingdom. An example of a classical model of evangelism is seen in Christ's encounter with the Samaritan woman at the well of Sychar (John 4:1-42). Jesus' Great Commission includes evangelism (Matthew 28:19-20, Mark 16:15, Luke 24:47) especially through preaching repentance and the forgiveness of sins. Paul wrote, "I am not ashamed of the gospel, because it is the power of God that brings salvation to everyone that believes..." (Romans 1:16) and "faith comes by hearing the word of God" (Romans 10:17). Evangelism occurs both by proclamation and by living out the truth of the gospel. It should be the goal of every evangelist and all believers.

Scholars in the field of evangelism have expressed the theology of evangelism in diverse ways. Walter Brueggemann an Old Testament scholar writing on evangelism argues that "the ground of evangelism is found in the gospel itself and not in any church condition or societal need" (Brueggemann, 1993, loc. 7). He proposes that "evangelism ...is 'doing the text' again, as our text and as 'news' addressed to us and waiting to be received, appropriated, and enacted in our own time and place" (Brueggemann, 1993, section 8). Doing the text means allowing the voice of the scriptural text to have a full say in our common life (Brueggemann, 1993, loc. 9). He views the drama played out in the Old Testament (God's promise to the nation of Israel, deliverance from slavery, and the gift of the land) as good news and as being re-enacted in God's victory over evil and sin in the New Testament, the proclamation of that victory in evangelism, and the appropriation of the message by those who accept the message. Thus, the gospel gives true meaning to the Old Testament drama. Connecting Brueggemann's theology of evangelism is Scot McKnight who argues that the gospel is "declaring the story of Israel as resolved in the story of Jesus" (McKnight 2011, Loc. 1143). He insists on the connection between the story of Israel and Jesus who fulfills and completes that story. For McKnight, our part today is seen in the call to believe, repent, and be baptized which is participation in the story of Jesus (McKnight 2011, Loc. 2016). Scott J. Jones on the theology of evangelism further argues that "the ministry of evangelism must be grounded in the love of God and neighbor" (Jones 2003, Loc. 166). This understanding connects the story of Israel and its call by God to love him and to love its neighbors (Deuteronomy 6:4,5; Luke 10:27). In agreement with Jones, we can effectively evangelize people if we truly love the Lord and love them as well. Paul's sufferings on account of seeking to evangelize the lost in II Corinthians 11:21-33 underscore the fact that evangelism is not an easy task. It takes love to effectively carry out this task. Jones further remarks that evangelizing non-Christian persons without loving them fully is equivalent to evangelizing poorly, and that loving them without evangelizing them is loving them poorly (Jones 2003, loc. 216). True Christian love should go beyond meeting only human needs to meet their spiritual needs as well.

The good news as seen by Darrell Bock (2010, p. 20) is the restoration of relationship with the living God that makes those who believe and have obtained forgiveness part of His family. God extended His love to mankind by sending His Son to die for the sins of the world; he initiated the relationship and accepted us as part of His family. This common relationship as sons and daughters of the Lord enables us to form communities of fellowship as people of God. The restoration of relationships and formation of a community of faith make us part of the Kingdom. William Abraham (1989), while connecting evangelism with the Kingdom, argues that evangelism should be understood primarily as initiation into the Kingdom of God. "We can best improve our thinking on evangelism by conceiving it as that set of intentional activities which is governed by the goal of initiating people into the kingdom of God for the first time" (Abraham 1989, loc. 1142). The word initiation can be confusing; therefore, Abraham explains it by saying, "to initiate someone into the kingdom of God is to admit that person into the eschatological rule of God through appropriate instruction, experiences, rites, and forms" (Abraham, 1989, loc. 1157). This definition and explanation rightly link evangelism with discipleship. Dallas Willard (2006) notes that the lack of discipleship in the Great Commission is a Great Omission. It is important to conclude the section on the theology of evangelism with the thoughts of Charles Arn (2003) who did very extensive research on evangelizing senior adults. He is an advocate of an approach to evangelism that is "disciple-oriented" rather than "decision-oriented." He sees the journey toward Christian faith as a process over time (Arn 2003, p. 85). With this approach, he believes senior adults will be more willing to participate in the journey of faith. The command in the Great Commission is for us to make disciples of Christ out of the people we win to Him. The command to reach people with the gospel includes the elderly, who should be won to Christ and become His disciples.

Understanding Senior Adults

Senior adults, as defined in this paper, are sixty years and above. However, they could include younger adults in countries or communities where the life expectancy is low. With advances in healthcare and medical science, the number of senior adults is growing, especially in the West. There has also been growth in some non-western countries. Oswald J. Sanders (1982) in his book, *Your Best Years: Staying Young While Growing Old*, gave the following statistics and projections about the swelling number of senior adults in the United States, which is similar to most countries in the west. He wrote,

> In 1850, only 2.5 percent of American citizens were over sixty-five. Today the proportion is 10 percent. Ten years ago; 4.4 percent were seventy-five years old or over. By the year 2000, the number could reach 6.9 percent. The United States today has 25 million people of sixty-five and over. If the present tendency toward a decreasing death rate continues, the number could increase to 38 million by the year 2000. The United States is not alone in this dilemma, similar conditions exist in Europe (Sanders 1982, 27).

The statistics about the growing number of senior adults agree with Arn's (2003) conclusion that "America is rapidly aging as the baby boomers are growing old, and our population is living longer." He calls this the "age wave" that "is ushering America into unfamiliar territory that has significant implications for the Church" (Arn, p. 10). The growing number of senior adults the world over requires a conscientious effort by practitioners of evangelism and mission to target senior adults as a special people group and win them to Christ. Sanders says, "Old age is just as important and meaningful a part of God's will as youth. God is every bit as interested in the old as in the young" (1982, p. 42). There are people who respond to the gospel in their old age and who use their influence to open the door for witness in their families, their communities, and other spheres of their influence.

Billy Graham (2011), discussing his age, admitted that as age increases, the energy of a person decreases, and everything becomes slower, even recovery from illnesses. It is good to hear him talk about the challenges of old age, "There is no doubt that catastrophic illnesses take their toll on the elderly. Just as our bodies age and decline, so do our minds. In reality, the two are closely connected; as we age, physical changes take place in our brains as well as the rest of our bodies, causing everything from mild memory loss to dementia and Alzheimer's disease" (Billy Graham 2011, p. 154). The writer, having done some participant observation studies with senior adults in 2020-2021, agrees with Billy Graham concerning the struggles the elderly encounter with their physical, mental, and emotional health. Anyone involved in reaching the senior adults with the gospel must know and understand these struggles and find a way to be of help to them.

A better description of the struggles of senior adults can be found in Solomon's description of old age in Ecclesiastes 12:1-7. The Zondervan Study Bible's (2015) commentary on the passage above pointed out three main ways of reading the passage: 1) the allegorical approach in which objects and activities in the passage represent the challenges of old age, 2) a literal reading which sees in the passage a description of death and dying, and 3) a symbolic reading which sees the images in the passage as similar to the language of the prophets. I will prefer the allegorical approach in this paper since we are dealing with the challenges of old age and how to evangelize senior adults within their context. The problem of aging is like twilight gloom; it is the dark side of life for many elderly people, a time of pain and regret. To some, it is a time of loneliness and even desertion. In Ecclesiastes, the arms and the hands which protect the body, as Solomon describes them, shake in old age. The failing memory of the elderly is depicted by the shaking of the head. The legs which are like the supporting pillars of the body become weak and the muscles decline and shrink, making stability a problem. The teeth, as grinders of food, get weak, loosen, and some or all are lost which makes chewing very difficult. The eyes become dim which sometimes results in blindness. Old age brings a loss of appetite and little is eaten. Senior adults have light sleep; a slight noise like the chirping of a bird may wake them up. Music does not make sense; ear pain and hearing loss may occur in old age. Senior adults fear heights because they can fall. In my experience with senior adults during the participant observation study, I recall times when they fell because they could not maintain their balance; sometimes such falls are devastating. Old age results in gray hair, though not all gray hair is due to old age. The end of the aging process is death. Despite these common phenomena, the aging process differs from person to person due to differences in genetic make-up, accessibility to healthcare, diet, rest, attitudes to old age, lifestyle, and the presence of joy and peace from the Holy Spirit, among many other factors.

Strategies for Evangelizing Senior Adults

Just as there are strategies for reaching children, youth, women, and others with the gospel, a strategy is also needed to effectively reach senior adults. "Effective outreach communicates the Good News in different ways to different 'people groups.' (Arn, 2003, p. 75). We need to consider some strategies for reaching the elderly with the gospel. In this section of the paper, we will discuss the why, the who, and the how of gerontic evangelism. This will help put the evangelists who desire to consider this ministry on track.

Why Evangelize Senior Adults?

There is a wide belief among practitioners of evangelism that most Christian conversions occur among children and younger adults. Charles Arn in one of his research findings said, "few Christian adults over age 65 indicate their conversion occurred later in life." Quoting one of his studies, he found that "only 7% of all Christian conversion occur after age 50; 1% after age 60..." (Arn, 30). The question is, if senior adults are not responsive to the gospel, why bother with them? Reacting to the claim that relatively few senior adults respond to the gospel, David Moore (2007) quoted Dr. William Day who believes that senior adults do not respond because they are not targeted for evangelism like the other groups. He said it is not likely that senior adults will make a profession of faith "unless intentional ministry is directed toward them" (p. 27). One of the objectives of this paper is to appeal for a more intentional effort for the evangelization of Senior Adults. Building upon the claim that senior adults can and do respond to the gospel is the claim of socioemotional selectivity theory which argues that "perception of time is inevitably linked to the selection and pursuit of social goals" (Carstensen & Isaacowitz, 1999, p. 166). The perception of the amount of time left in life can be a motivation for senior adults to embrace Christ and change their ways.

Arn (2003) presented the following reasons for pursuing the evangelization of senior adults as follows: Senior adults are close to eternity, receptive, care about others, have more available time, are loyal to the church, are geographically stable, and give more money to the church (Arn, 2003, pp. 76-78). In addition to the reasons advocated by Arn, as a participant observer who interacted with both the elderly and their relations, I wish to advance the following reasons in this paper.

First, the scripture says that it is not God's will that any should perish, but that all should be saved (2 Peter 3:9). Senior adults of all races, cultures, economic, and social statuses who do not know the Lord are precious souls that need salvation. Unlike some religions or cultures where good or influential elders just grow old, die, and join their ancestors, it is not so in the Christian faith. The scripture clearly states that "the soul that sins shall die" (Ezekiel 18:20), hence the need to rescue the perishing who are headed toward eternal damnation.

Second, another reason for considering the urgency of evangelizing senior adults is that some seniors may not live long before they are called to glory. Our joy will know no bounds when we meet these souls in heaven who narrowly escaped hell because of our faithfulness in witnessing Christ to them.

Third, in some cultures, senior adults are highly revered and respected. Oswald Sanders gave this example, "In Oriental culture, age is equated with wisdom. In countries like Japan, the elderly have a respected status and enjoy high prestige. A person is valued for his intrinsic character more than for what he achieves" (Sanders, 1982, p. 22). This respected status is enjoyed by senior adults in most African cultures and in many other cultures around the world. When such influential senior adults are won to Christ, they may use their influence for the evangelization of their families, communities, clans, and even people groups. Some seniors are gatekeepers of their communities or tribes.

It should be noted that in patriarchal societies, the elderly men should be the target while in matriarchal societies elderly women should be targeted. In my discussions in the Tri-State region of Appalachia, I found out that women have a special influence. This was revealed in an informal discussion in April 2022 with Bobby Mercer of Tri-State Bible College, South Point Ohio, USA. If the evangelist understands this, then he or she should target the elderly women who can be a doorway to reaching the men and other members of their community or society.

Fourth, in the introduction, we saw that the number of senior adults in different parts of the world is increasing. This growing number provides a reasonable justification for why missionaries, evangelists, and churches should consider them as a target group for outreach beyond just caring for their physical needs.

Fifth, saved senior adults who have done very bad things in the past might right their wrongs which will make a positive impact on the community or society and that will give credence to the gospel witness.

Sixth, In some cultures, seniors take care of little children. Children in some cultures gather around grandparents for moral and religious instruction. Because of this, senior adults who are believers can be a great resource for evangelizing children, hence providing hope for the future of the Christian faith.

Having discussed why senior adults should be targeted for evangelism, it is important now to discuss the kind of persons suitable for the evangelization of senior adults.

Who Should Evangelize Senior Adults?

For a strategic and effective outreach to senior adults, the person who should evangelize them is very important. Just as Robert Coleman (2014) observed, people are the most important element of the strategy of Christ for winning the world. "Remarkable as it may seem, Jesus started to gather these men before he ever organizes an evangelistic campaign or even preached a sermon in public. Men were to be his method of winning the world to God" (Coleman 2014, loc. 21). To reach the elderly effectively, the characteristics of men and women who will do the work are important. From my participant observation with the seniors, I have been able to come up with the following qualities for evangelists that will effectively reach senior adults with the gospel.

First, the evangelist must be born again and be filled with the Holy Spirit. One cannot give what one does not have. It is saved people, empowered by the Holy Spirit, who should be evangelizing.

Second, another necessary quality of a person who desires to reach senior adults with the gospel is love. Loving the Lord and loving people is an indispensable quality for an evangelist. The elderly, in particular those who are unsaved, require extraordinary love in order to cope with the changes taking place in their minds, bodies, and overall health. The unsaved senior especially needs to be loved, and this love must flow from Christ through the life of the evangelist.

Third, an evangelist who wants to reach senior adults must be a listener. Elderly people love to tell their stories, whether they be of success or regret, and they need someone willing to listen to them. These stories can serve as a bridge to connect the seniors with the gospel. Wise use of this resource can result in the successful witnessing of Christ to senior adults.

Fourth, patience is also one of the necessary qualities for an evangelist of senior adults to possess. Patience is especially helpful when the senior adults repeat the same story or when they quickly forget what they were told. Likewise, patience is also useful when one must help them do routine activities or when they sometimes behave like children.

Fifth, anyone reaching out to senior adults must study and understand the problems of old age. This will help him or her to build rapport with them.

Sixth, because of failing strength and illnesses, senior adults need care. The evangelist must be caring. Elderly people need to know you care for them and they appreciate any gestures that demonstrate this care. Our love is manifested in the ways we care for them.

Seventh, an evangelist to senior adults must have compassion for the lost. He or she must care for the eternal destiny of the senior adults.

Eighth, an effective evangelist to senior adults must be a good disciple-maker. Evangelism that is only after conversions is not fitting for senior adults. A good disciple-maker should be able to go over and over the same lessons with the elderly because they can easily forget the material.

Ninth, an evangelist to the elderly must be respectful. Senior adults want to be respected; therefore, any disrespect can close doors for evangelism. One must study and understand what constitutes respect or disrespect to the elderly in the culture of the targeted people group.

Tenth, another quality needed is the means and ability to physically visit the elderly. Some of them feel lonely because of mobility limitations. Visits which allow them plenty of time to talk can open a door for witness. God needs men and women to commit themselves to reaching the elderly with the gospel. This list of qualities needed to evangelize senior adults provides the would-be evangelist with the necessary tools to start.

How to Evangelize Senior Adults?

During my experience of participant observation, I was able to observe the following approaches to reaching the elderly.

First, enlisting and training men and women for ministry to the elderly is essential.

Second, one needs to approach the elderly respectfully with love. Again, learning what constitutes respect or disrespect to elders in their cultural context is required.

Third, listening is an important skill for reaching the elderly. Elderly people have stories to tell us about their life. Our ability to set aside time to sit and listen to their stories is a great blessing to them. Some of the stories may be repeated several times in the same sitting, but we must listen nonetheless. We should wisely use those stories as stepping stones for gospel witness. We should also be able to ask questions that will connect elderly people with their past, especially with regard to family, profession, friendships, and their likes and dislikes, in addition to asking questions that will prepare them for the future.

Fourth, although some elderly people may want to maintain their independence, many have needs that they cannot meet alone. Some have been out of work or retired for a long time and have no children to care for them. Some have been deserted by their children. Their needs may include food, clothes, shelter, rent, utilities, healthcare, security, household chores, transportation, or running errands. The light of Christ shines in dark places where needs are met with love and care. We become the proverbial hands of Jesus reaching out to meet their needs.

Fifth, a ministry strategy of reaching the elderly includes sharing the gospel message with them, perhaps through Bible study (individually or in small groups) or through praying for their needs, which is often appreciated by people who are not believers. Other dimensions of ministry include counseling and literature evangelism; some old people enjoy reading and may appreciate good Christian titles.

Sixth, in oral communities, storytelling, especially Bible stories, can be a good strategy to reach the elderly. As we listen to their stories, we can also share relevant Bible stories that demonstrate a connection with what they have experienced.

Seventh, caregiving: a church or Christian organization can establish a caregiving center where the elderly, both believers and unbelievers, can receive care, through which the gospel message can be communicated to the unsaved. Homecare can also be established as a ministry to the elderly and can be used as an avenue for witnessing. Believers can take jobs in eldercare facilities or homecare organizations and work faithfully in love to share Christ by word and deed.

Eighth, Charles Arn (2003) suggests training senior adults who are Christians to share their faith and to become effective disciple-makers. This is important because "older people not only interact with few people, but they also interact primarily with people who are well-known to them" (Carstensen & Isaacowitz, 1999, p. 169). This underscores the importance of equipping them to reach the senior adults in their immediate and extended circle of family and friends.

Conclusion

The primary objective of this paper is to challenge Christians and the church to reach the elderly with the Gospel, demonstrating how the elderly are precious to God. I wish to conclude this article with the words of David Moore who said, "the lack of evangelism which targets today's seniors is a growing crisis. The number of unsaved seniors will continue to expand unless today's churches and believers intentionally evangelize these needful individuals that God loves and desires to be part of His kingdom for eternity." (Moore, 2007, p. 23). Winning the elderly has the potential of opening more doors for witnessing and is thus strategic for the advancement of the gospel. Hence, all scriptural strategies should be used and guided by the Holy Spirit to bring these precious souls to the Kingdom.

References

Abraham, W. J. (1989). *The logic of evangelism.* Wm B. Eerdmans Publishing Co.

Arn, C. (2003). *White unto harvest: Evangelizing today's seniors.* Institute for American Church Growth

Bock, D. L. (2010). *Real lost gospel: Reclaiming the gospel as good news.* B&H Publishing Group

Brueggemann, W. (1993). *Biblical perspectives on evangelism: Living in a three storied universe.* Abingdon Press.

Carstensen, L. L., and Isaacowitz, D. M. (1999). Taking time seriously: A theory of socioemotional selectivity" *American Psychologist, 54*(3), 165-181.

Cire, B. (2016). World's older population grows dramatically. In *National Institutes of Health (NIH) News Release* (March 2016). https://www.nia.nih.gov/news/worlds-older-population-grows-dramatically

Coleman, R. E. (2014). *The master plan of evangelism.* Revell

Graham, B. (2011). *Nearing home: Life, faith, and finishing.* Thomas Nelson

Jones, S. J. (2003). *The evangelistic love of God and neighbor.* Abingdon Press

McKnight, S. (2011). *The King Jesus gospel: The original good news revisited.* Zondervan

Moore, D. E. (2007). Senior adult evangelism. *Journal of the American Society for Church Growth, 18*(3), 23-35.

NIV Zondervan Study Bible. (2015). D. A. Carson et al. eds. Commentary on Ecclesiastes 12:1-8. Zondervan.

Ray, D. (1979). *The forty plus handbook: The fine art of growing older.* Word Publishing Group.

Sanders, O. J. (1982). *Your best years: Staying young while growing.* Moody Press

Willard, D. (2006). *The great omission: Rediscovering Jesus' essential teachings on discipleship.* HarperCollins

Williamson, J. B. (1980). *Aging and society: Introduction to social gerontology.* Holt, Rinehart, and Winston.

Wright, N. T. (2015). *Simply good news: Why the gospel is news and what makes it good.* HarperCollins Publishers.

About the Author

Yakubu Jakada, PhD, has served the Lord as a rural evangelist in his home country, Nigeria, as a Church Pastor, and as a Seminary Lecturer. He is now an adjunct faculty of Tri-State Bible College, South Point, Ohio, USA. Email: jakaday86@gmail.com

GREAT COMMISSION
RESEARCH JOURNAL
2022, Vol. 14(2) 115-131

Not Interested: Communicating with Those Indifferent to the Gospel

W. Jay Moon
Asbury Theological Seminary

Presidential message at the 2022 Annual Conference of the Great Commission Research Network held in Orlando, Florida. Parts of this address are based on Moon and Simon (2021).

Picture a visit to a university campus as you stroll through a dining hall and talk with people you meet. When you bring up questions about faith, you hear responses such as, "Religion is irrelevant to my life and neither good nor bad," "My life got busier," and "Church was boring and there was no need for it." These are actual comments from surveys conducted by Bethany Moon on the American University campus in Washington, DC, in 2020.

These students are not hostile to faith discussions. Instead, they are simply *indifferent*. They often don't see the relevance of being part of a church, and they don't see the purpose behind faith either. So how do you engage people that seem to be indifferent to faith and church? Did Jesus ever engage those who were indifferent? This article explores three different worldviews and discusses the emerging worldview of indifference. Then, I provide some guidance from Jesus' approach to those who were indifferent in his day.

In a Previous Generation

Evangelism in a previous generation was similar to a revival meeting. When you engaged people in faith discussions, you were trying to bring them back to a faith they once had, or their parents had. At least there was some Christian memory or awareness that the evangelist wanted to awaken. This assumption is no longer true in many settings, such as school, work, and leisure activities. Today, you are more likely to engage people of different faith systems. You may encounter a Buddhist, Hindu, Muslim, or even Wiccan with all kinds of different varieties and combinations in between, including those who are indifferent. A research project over the last eight years has been conducted in partnership with Knox fellowship and Asbury Theological Seminary in order to identify the complexities and opportunities for faith sharing in this generation. Cohorts of students meet for eight weeks to prepare to engage people of different faiths. During the last week, students invite unchurched and de-churched people to a meal in order to engage them in faith conversations.

Cliff Jumping

During the first week of the cohort, I tell students that, eight weeks from now, you will be in faith discussion with perhaps Muslims, Buddhists, and Wiccans. A look of fear spreads across their face, almost like I just asked them to jump off a cliff! To be honest, I have done some cliff jumping in the past, so I know that fear. When I leaped off of a 60-foot cliff, the fear immediately arose and accelerated each second in the air. The funny thing about jumping off of a high cliff is that you get a lot of time to think as you are in midair! As the water is coming toward you, thoughts arise like, "How did I get here?" and "How is this going to end?" Students often feel the same way when asked to enter into faith discussions with those from other worldviews. During the first week of the cohort, they are fearful about how to get into faith conversations and how will it end. After training over 500 participants in these cohorts, we have noticed an increase in the students' confidence (from 39% to 87%) and competence (from 31% to 93%; Moon, 2017). I will share some of what we learned in order to help people overcome their fears. First, though, some definitions are needed to establish some common ground and plot the way forward (See Moon & Simons, 2021, for a more in-depth discussion).

Definitions

Intercultural evangelism is "The process of *worldview change* that *initiates* people into Christian *discipleship* through *culturally relevant starting points*." The goal is to initiate people into discipleship.

Evangelism seeks to change the worldview and not simply add another cognitive assertion on top of an existing worldview (more on that later). In addition, as opposed to evangelism and discipleship being two separate tasks, this is really one long process where the goal of evangelism, as Billy Abraham (1989) told us in the *Logic of Evangelism*, is to initiate people into a long journey of discipleship. Finding culturally relevant starting points is crucial since I assume that God is already starting a conversation with everybody you meet, even those who don't recognize it yet. The role of the evangelist is to catch up on that conversation and keep that moving towards Christ. Evangelists need to listen well to identify the unique starting point that God has already initiated with that person. Within different worldviews, those starting points are often also very different, although there are recognizable patterns.

Missiologist Paul Hiebert (2008, pp. 25-26) defines worldview as "The foundational cognitive, affective, and evaluative assumptions and frameworks a group of people makes about the nature of reality which they use to order their lives. It encompasses people's images or maps of the reality of all things that they use for living their lives." Note that this definition includes the things you think about, but it's also the things that you love and value. James K. A. Smith (2016) is fond of saying, "You become what you love" – not simply what you think. If somebody comes to faith and they just change what they think, but they don't change what they love, then what happens? Since they still love the things in the world, they still act like people in the world! Worldviews then affect what people think, but also what they love, and how they evaluate decisions. Evangelism needs to engage a person at the worldview level.

Worldviews are like different colored lenses: If you wear blue-tinted glasses, then everything you see has a blue tint. Worldviews are so important then because they color everything we think, love, and value. As a result, understanding someone's worldview gives the evangelist a helpful starting point concerning where God is already having a conversation with someone. This is precisely why a "one size fits all" evangelism approach often falls short: God has different conversations with people through the different worldviews they inhabit.

Guilt/Justice Worldview

In a previous generation, aspiring evangelists were often taught a gospel formula similar to this: all of us have sinned. Because of the guilt our sin has produced, we are separated from God. Jesus takes the guilt of sin upon himself. Like a judge slamming the gavel down, God says, "Not guilty!" The meaning of the cross is that Jesus takes our guilt upon himself; therefore, justice has been performed and we stand justified before God guilt-free. Ninety-nine percent of the time when I hear an evangelistic message on the radio, it follows this type of approach. It assumes that people have internal guilt and that the cross brings justice before God to remove that guilt. This makes sense for a worldview that views guilt as the result of sin. What happens, though, if guilt is not the primary response to sin? In a pluralist society, people do not always have guilt; instead, they may respond to sin with shame, fear, or even indifference. Without realizing it, we have put on a straitjacket that restricts our explanation of the gospel. While that straight jacket fits for one worldview, such as a guilt/justice worldview, it is terribly inadequate for other worldviews. Instead of assuming that everybody has guilt and therefore we can present salvation in terms of justice, what if there are other starting points to explain the gospel?

New Testament scholar Brenda Colijn (2010, 14–16) explains,

> The New Testament does not develop a systematic doctrine of salvation. Instead, it presents us with a variety of pictures taken from different perspectives. ... the variety of images attests to both the complexity of the human problem and its solution .... Each image is a picture of salvation from one perspective, posing and answering one set of questions.

She describes twelve different images that are different images of salvation from various perspectives. Each image poses another set of questions and provides another set of responses. In short, these different worldviews describe where God has started a conversation with people about how they regard the effect of sin to explain the significance of the cross for them. Missiologist Craig Ott (2014) explains that evangelists should "begin with a biblical analogy that has the most common ground with the hearers' worldview."

Fear/Power Worldview

What does it look like to engage a different worldview that is not based upon guilt/justice? When I lived in Ghana, West Africa, I labored for a solid year to learn the language well enough to explain the gospel to the Builsa people. I was excited to finally be in the position to share the gospel! I started off using the same formula explained above that assumes people have guilt that Jesus can remove to restore their just standing before God. At the end of my explanation, they looked at me and said, "Well, that's interesting - but not really."

I was shocked.

How can the gospel be of little interest? I did not realize that I had limited the gospel presentation to a guilt/justice worldview whereas the Builsa had an entirely different worldview. To get a sense of their worldview, look at Figure 1.

Figure 1. *Builsa at the Fiok Festival*

This event is called the *Fiok* festival where the Builsa commemorate when they repelled the Muslim slave raiders from the north who previously conducted a jihad and captured the Builsa as slaves to sell them to other tribes, eventually ending in the transatlantic slave trade. This is similar to the U.S. Fourth of July celebration where we commemorate our independence. Look at what they're wearing on their smocks: These are pieces of leather that they took to an earth shrine called the *tengbain* to collect dirt that is sewn inside to give them spiritual protection. The fear of spiritual forces, witchcraft, juju, or the evil eye lurk just below the surface in the Builsa culture. They don't look at the effect of sin as being internal guilt; instead, the effect of sin has produced fear. This is an important distinction.

In Genesis 3, God seeks out Adam and Eve after they sinned. In response to God's calling him, Adam responds, "I heard you in the garden, and I was afraid because I was naked; so I hid." (Genesis 3:10). In other words, one of the first results of sin was fear. When I explained the gospel to the Builsa in terms of how the cross addresses their fear (and not only guilt), there was a totally different response. The gospel made much more sense when focusing on God's restoration of power to those in fear, using a gospel presentation similar to the following: In the beginning, our first ancestors were close to God. Once they disobeyed God, humans were afraid, and God put a curse upon humanity. God promised that one day the seed of the woman would bring someone who would crush the head of the devil to remove the fear of witchcraft, evil eye, juju, and everything else. In the fullness of time, God sent his own son named Jesus to remove that curse. When the Builsa heard this good news, they often responded, "Tell me more!" They recognized that the gospel is the power of God for salvation. Instead of simply a good way to remove guilt, Jesus offers the power of God to overcome fear. That is a very different starting point to share the gospel since the worldview is fear/power.

Shame/Honor Worldview

What happens when you engage people from a worldview that does not recognize the effects of sin as producing guilt or fear? Many cultures regard the result of sin as producing shame. While guilt is an inner individual response to sin, shame is an outward collective response to sin. Going back to the story of Adam and Eve in the garden, before they ate the fruit, Genesis 2:25 describes the happy couple this way, "Adam and his wife were both naked, and they felt no shame." Once they sin, though, "they realized they were naked; so they sewed fig leaves together and made coverings for themselves" (Genesis 3:7). This is when shame entered the human experience.

One of the effects of sin then is shame (not simply guilt and fear). This worldview recognizes that shame is like a credit card: You can add to it (by saving face) or subtract from it (by losing face). In this worldview, those who are shamed are not looking for justice or power; instead, they are looking for honor. In the shame/honor worldview, Jesus offers honor to restore people to the family of God. The prodigal son story in Luke 15 provides a good gospel explanation since the son's honor is restored (signified by the ring and the robe) as a member of the family again.

Figure 2 summarizes the discussion so far concerning three different worldviews. Since sin results in a different response in each worldview, the significance of Jesus' life, death, and resurrection is viewed differently. The image of salvation that is most relevant to them is also very different. A relationship with God is then viewed differently as well.

	Worldview		
	Guilt/Justice	*Shame/Honor*	*Fear/Power*
Typical location:	West (N. America, Europe)	East (Middle East, N. Africa, Asia)	South (sub-Saharan Africa, tribal, Caribbean)
Sin's result:	separation/guilt	shame	fear/curse/bondage
Solution in Jesus:	payment/substitute	honor restored, cleansed	deliverance
Image of salvation:	courtroom/justice	relationship, cleansing	power, freedom
Relationship with God:	Judge who declares, "Not guilty!"	Father who restores honor	Creator who protects and delivers

Figure 2. *Evangelism differences among three common worldviews*

What happens though when people do not exhibit the typical responses to sin? Returning to our university students, how do you engage someone who does not express guilt, fear, or shame?

Indifference/Belonging with Purpose Worldview

This is another unique starting point that is not simply limited to North America: It also includes the former Communist bloc countries, as well as other post-Christian contexts that have been affected by secularization. This is a growing demographic so we cannot simply ignore those in this worldview; instead, we need to understand and engage their worldview. Again, we can assume that God is already having a conversation with those who are indifferent, even if they are not willing to admit it.

In our research at Asbury Theological Seminary, we kept running into people whose worldview did not fall into the categories of guilt/justice, shame/honor, or fear/power. Eventually, we realized what sociology professor Steve Bruce (2002:42) described, "The end point of secularization is not atheism but religious indifference." During our research, we noticed that those in the addictive community are often open to the fear/power worldview discussion. In addition, the shame/honor worldview seems to be on the rise among people connected to social media since shame needs an audience and social media provides a large audience. But indifference was the dominant worldview.

To understand this indifferent worldview a bit more, a 2019 National Study of American Twentysomethings (NSAT) was conducted (Clydesdale and Garces-Foley, 2019). They surveyed 1,880 young adults, conducted 200 interviews, interviewed 49 religiously unaffiliated ("nones"), and studied 11 congregations and parachurch ministries that were effective at reaching the twenty-somethings. Figure 3 summarizes the religious affiliation of the twenty-somethings studied.

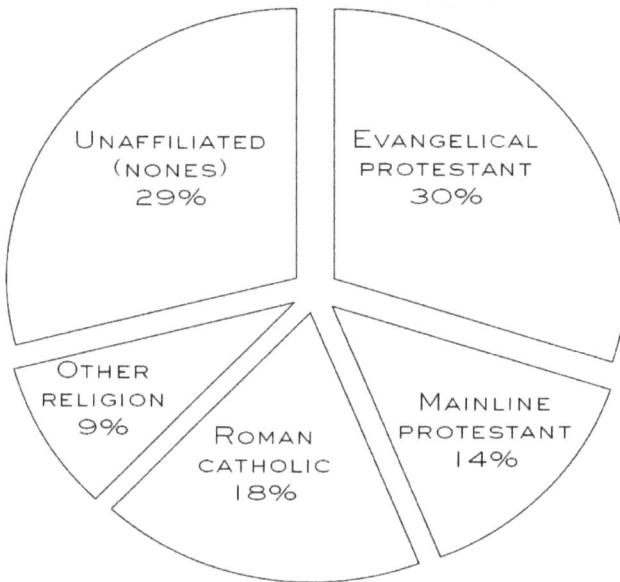

Figure 3. *Religious Affiliation of Twenty-Somethings*

This is how these 20 Somethings were grouped. The largest group of 30% were evangelical Protestants, 14% were mainline Protestants, 18% were Roman Catholics, and other religions were 9%. Look at the unaffiliated (nones) who make up 29%. This is almost the largest group. This is significant not simply due to the large percentage but also because it is growing rapidly. The NSAT drilled down into this group of unaffiliated (nones) to understand their religious perspectives further, as summarized in Figure 4.

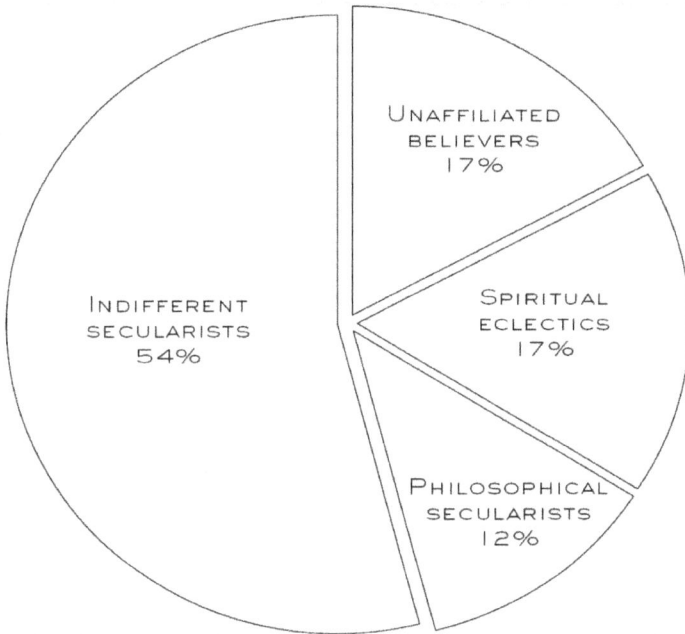

Figure 4. *Types of Unaffiliated Twenty-Something (Nones)*

Seventeen percent of the group are unaffiliated believers, meaning they still consider themselves Christians, but they just don't see the relevance of going to church. Seventeen percent are spiritual eclectics. Missiologists use the term syncretists for those who combine some Christian practices with practices of other religions such as Buddhism or a local folk religion, forming an eclectic mix. Those 12% who are philosophical secularists compose a rather small group. These are the ones who philosophically have convinced themselves that secularism makes the most sense. Incidentally, Tim Keller (2016) described a 'crisis of secularism' that is actually growing where people recognize that secularism has so many gaps in meaning. Since secularism alone cannot address these questions, many conclude secularism is not a very tenable position after all.

The largest group though, by far, is the indifferent secularists at 54%. This demographic is one that we need to understand and engage. Where is a good starting point for gospel conversations with the indifferent crowd?

John Stott, in a previous era, said post-moderns are often yearning for three things:

1. Community—a sense that in a fragmenting world and society they *belong* to a family.
2. Significance—a sense that they are meaningful, have *purpose*, and make a difference.
3. Transcendence—a sense or a connection with what is beyond immediate and material things and beings (Pocock, Van Rheenen, and McConnell 2005, 116).

I added the italics to draw attention to the desire for belonging as well as purpose. They want a community where they can belong, like a family. They also want some significance where they find a purpose. In addition, they want transcendence where they're connected to something beyond just themselves and their own material world.

A more recent study was conducted by Beth Severson (2020) among emerging adults (ages 18-35) that found they will often come to faith by one of these three pathways:

1. They experience compelling *community*.
2. They *make a difference* through service or leadership.
3. They receive mentoring or leadership development.

Again, I added italics to emphasize the desire for belonging (community) as well as purpose (making a difference).

To summarize, those who are indifferent are often yearning for belonging with purpose. They want to belong to a community that feels like a family. In this community, they want to live for a purpose that is bigger than themselves in order to make a difference in the world. Since that is their yearning, perhaps that is the place God is already conversing with them, which indicates this is a good starting point. Is there any biblical precedent for this?

Indifference in Jesus' Day

The story of Zacchaeus in Luke 19 can be of help. He was a chief tax collector, which indicates he was not even allowed into the temple. As a result, he was indifferent to the religious system of his day. When Jesus encounters Zacchaeus and visits him at his house, Jesus did not discuss guilt, shame, or fear. Jesus brought the disciples with him. During that meal, Zacchaeus feels like he belongs in this community.

Experiencing a sense of belonging, Zacchaeus stands up and says, "Look, Lord! Here and now I give half of my possessions to the poor, and if I have cheated anybody out of anything, I will pay back four times the amount" (Luke 19:8).

Jesus then quickly replies, "Today salvation has come to this house" (Luke 19:9). In other words, as Zacchaeus recognizes he belongs in this community, he is now given a new purpose for his life and work. This "belonging with purpose" is a good starting point for faith discussions with those who are indifferent. Figure 2 is revised to add this additional emerging worldview, as shown in Figure 5.

	Worldview			
	Guilt/Justice	*Shame/Honor*	*Fear/Power*	*Indifference/ Belonging with Purpose*
Typical location:	West (N. America, Europe)	East (Middle East, N. Africa, Asia)	South (sub-Saharan Africa, tribal, Caribbean)	Post-religious
Sin's result:	guilt/ separation	shame	fear/curse/ bondage	indifference
Solution in Jesus:	payment/ substitute	honor restored, cleansed	deliverance	belonging with purpose
Image of salvation:	courtroom/ justice	relationship, cleansing	power, freedom	coming home
Relation-ship with God:	Judge who declares, "Not guilty!"	Father who restores honor	Creator who protects & delivers	Family who welcomes you home

Figure 5. *Evangelism and Four Worldviews*

To summarize these four worldviews, sin results in guilt, thus Jesus provides justice for those in the guilt/justice worldview. This is true and biblical, but it is not the whole part of the story. Sin also produces fear and Jesus provides the power of God for salvation for those in the fear/power worldview. In addition, sin produces shame and Jesus restores the honor of those in the shame/honor worldview by making them members of the family of God. In the right-hand column of Figure 5, I added the fourth emerging worldview that acknowledges that sin can also produce indifference. Like in Zacchaeus' life, Jesus offers belonging with purpose. The image of salvation that corresponds to God's conversation with those that are indifferent is of someone coming home. They may be coming home to a family they had previously strayed from or to a family they never had but had always longed for. That's the image for those who are indifferent: Jesus invites them to come home to a community that offers purpose. That image is a starting point for conversation with those who are indifferent.

A Mixing Board

So how is this fleshed out? So far, I have discussed these four worldviews as discrete worldviews. In practice, they are often integrated. Oftentimes, people have one or two of these worldviews in their background. As you listen to them in conversations, you can discover which worldview is operating in order to know where to start gospel conversations. Along the way, you may notice another worldview, so you adjust, similar to moving the sliders on a mixing board that balances musical signals.

For example, when we were conversing with a millennial named Alice, she said, "You know, I used to go to a church, but it's been a long time, and didn't see the use of it." So we started to engage her in indifference by describing how Jesus offers belonging and purpose. After the conversation progressed for a while, she said, "Well, right now, I'm really involved in Wicca, and I hope that's going to help me."

At this point, the conversation moved over to the fear/power worldview. When someone is engaged in Wicca, it's usually not just due to curiosity. Oftentimes, there is something that's gripping them that they are hoping to overpower. It may be something as mundane as getting a date for Friday night, or maybe something more serious, like abuse in the home. They are often locked in fear and what they want to hear is not a Christ who simply offers justice, honor, or belonging. They are crying out for power to break free from what is locking them in fear. Eventually, the discussion gravitated toward the fear/power worldview and Alice was very interested to hear what we had to say. She eventually went to church with one of us. Figure 6 portrays how Alice is influenced by these two worldviews and how the discussion focused on the areas where God is having a conversation with her (not simply where God is conversing with me). Alice's example provides insight into personal conversations. But what about on a larger scale?

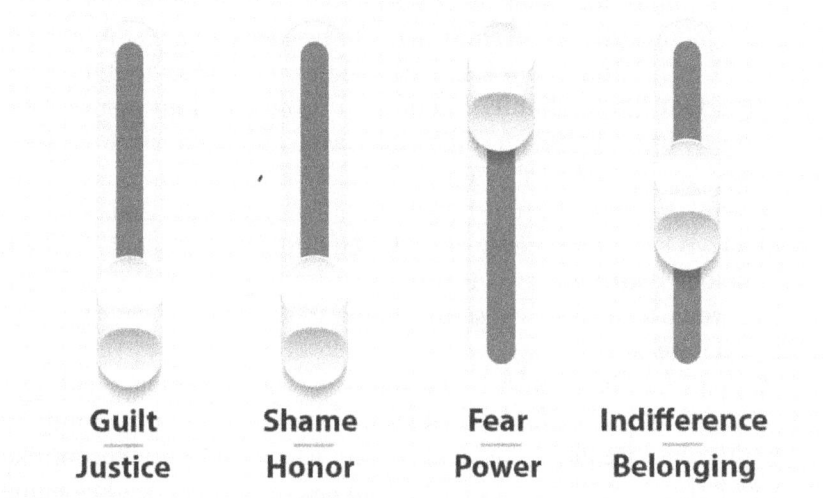

Guilt   Shame   Fear   Indifference

Justice   Honor   Power   Belonging

Figure 6. *The Influence of a Combination of Worldviews on Alice*

Chi Alpha at American University

If you have conversations with students at American University in Washington, DC, you will quickly realize that American University is not a hotbed of religious conservatism! Instead, students are often indifferent secularists. A Chi Alpha chapter (a student ministry associated with Assemblies of God) was formed to reach these students. Their website says, "Jesus. Purpose. Community." They recognize that for the indifferent people whom they are engaging, a good starting point is belonging (community) with purpose. So here is how they embody this belonging with purpose.

Their biggest outreach occurs at the beginning of the year during Welcome Week. They train students that if someone recognizes seven people in a group, they feel like they belong. As soon as they meet somebody, they introduce that person to others in the Chi Alpha group. When newcomers connect with seven Chi Alpha folks, they start to feel like they belong to the community. In addition, they hosted racial reconciliation meetings on campus, which is one way to demonstrate their purpose. Incidentally, while the American University administration doesn't often provide encouragement for the Chi Alpha group, they came to the Chi Alpha leadership to express their appreciation for the racial reconciliation meetings. No other group on campus has the racial or ethnic background to make it happen, nor did any have the desire or capacity to make it happen.

The Chi Alpha focus for evangelism is to invite people into small groups so that people have a community to belong to, which often leads to belief. The Chi Alpha students made statements such as "Authenticity is so important," "Christianity is not a 'to do list' or four steps," "We moved away from the Four Spiritual Laws approach since it feels inauthentic and impersonal," "Formulas feel like a fortune cookie," and "People want genuine relationships with others and with God." An AU student who is not yet a believer said, "When I think about people who are more religious than I am or if I were to have a reason to start going to church, it would be to have that sense of community. It's one of my favorite things about the church."

Let that sink in a bit. Here's someone who is unchurched and indifferent. He is looking for belonging. He is longing for a community to belong where he feels like he has come home. What could a church look like that would recognize this emerging worldview of indifference/belonging with purpose and then engage them in Christian community?

Kahaila Coffee

In London, England, church planter Paul Unsworth said that 20,000 people come by his street every Sunday morning with no Christian witness at all. There's somebody on the street corner talking about true Islam, so to speak, but there's no Christian witness there. So, Paul opened Kahaila coffee shop that also offers deserts and sandwiches. Paul said, "I've had more spiritual conversations with people in a week than I had working in a church for a whole year...people that don't know anything about Jesus."

Paul uses this business as a venue for the church plant. This is an example of an entrepreneurial church plant (ECP; Moon & Long, 2018) where communities of Christ followers are formed among unchurched or de-churched people in the marketplace. For some like Paul, this means starting a business. For others, they use an existing business as a venue for the church plant. There are several examples of this throughout the world. Paul's church gathers on Wednesday nights in the coffee shop space with about 35 people in attendance around 7 PM. Paul explained, "We need to find out how to form community. This is why we chose a coffee shop. It is a third space where people share life. We aim to build community in the café."

As a result of the proceeds of the coffee shop, they are training and employing vulnerable women as well as setting up a safe home for women. Some of their proceeds are also used for a prison visitation ministry in the neighborhood. They have combined belonging with purpose in order to address those who are indifferent. This is a starting point for Paul to catch up on conversations that God is having in the secular London culture.

The Next Step?

We have been discussing the emerging worldview of indifference and how Jesus offers belonging with purpose to those with this worldview as a starting point to discern how God has been speaking to them. It should be noted that this is a process; indifferent people coming to Jesus can take a fair amount of time. In empathetic dialogue, a question to consider is, "What is the next step for this person to come to faith?" As painful as it is to say, oftentimes their next step is not to invite them to a church. That's hard to accept since I wish they would come to church right away. For those who are indifferent though, several smaller steps may be necessary before they will come to your church.

One student put it to me this way. Suppose there's an imam who came to you and said, "I'd like you to come to my mosque on Friday. We have really good teaching that will help you and your family. We have a really nice building and lots of programs for the different needs of the community." Would you go to worship at that mosque? I had to admit, there's really nothing he could say that would get me into that mosque. That's when the student said, "That's how a lot of millennials feel about the church for various reasons."

The question to ask about the indifferent group is not "How do we get them to a church right away?" A more strategic question may be, "What is their next step in faith?" We can often arrive at answers to this by considering:

1. How do we create community they can join?
2. How do we create a place where they can belong?
3. What larger purpose can we offer them?
4. How can we invite them into a larger story that has purpose beyond their individual smaller story?

Eventually, we pray they will become a part of the church, but it may take some time.

Conclusion

Sadhu Sundar Sing, a beloved Christian from India, told a story of a high caste man in India who collapsed from heat exhaustion while waiting on a railway station platform (Seamands, 1981). Somebody ran over quickly and took a cup, filled it with water, and offered it to the man.

He refused to drink it.

Even though he was thirsty, and he needed some water, he refused. They noticed he had his own cup on the seat. So, they took his cup, filled it with water, and offered it to him.

He drank all of it.

Then Sundar Sing would say to his audience, 'This is what I have been trying to say to you missionaries from abroad. You have been offering the water of life to the people of India in a foreign cup, and we have been slow to receive it. If you will offer it in our own cup, we are much more likely to accept it."

To reach those who are indifferent to the gospel, we need to engage in empathetic listening in order to catch up on God's conversation with them. Instead of offering the gospel in the cup of the guilt/justice worldview, the emerging worldview of indifference/belonging with purpose is both biblical and more suited to their context. That is a cup that offers both refreshing water and satisfies their yearning.

References

Abraham, W. (1989). *The logic of evangelism*. Wm. B. Eerdmans.

Bruce, S. (2002). *God Is dead: Secularization in the West*. Wiley-Blackwell.

Clydesdale, T., & Garces-Foley, K. (2019). *The twentysomething soul: Understanding the religious and secular lives of American young adults*. Oxford University Press.

Colijn, B. (2010). *Images of salvation in the New Testament*. IVP Academic.

Hiebert, P. (2008). *Transforming worldviews: An anthropological understanding of how people change*. Baker Academic.

Keller, T. (2016). *Making sense of God: Finding God in the modern world*. Penguin.

Moon, W. J., ed. (2017). *Practical evangelism for the 21st century*. Glossa House & Digi-Books.

Moon, W. J., & Simon, B. (2021). *Effective intercultural evangelism: Good news in a diverse world*. InterVarsity Press.

Moon, W. J., Long, F., eds. (2018). *Entrepreneurial church planting: Innovative approaches to engage the marketplace*. Glossa House & Digi-Books.

Moreau, A. S., Campbell, E., & Greener, S. (2014). *Effective intercultural communication: A Christian perspective*. Encountering Mission Series. Baker Academic.

Ott, C. (2014). The power of biblical metaphors for the contextualized communication of the gospel. *Missiology 42*(4), 357–74.

Pocock, M., Van Rheenen, G., & McConnell, D. (2005). *The changing face of world missions: Engaging contemporary issues and trends*. Encountering Mission Series. Baker Academic.

Seamands, J. T. (1981). *Tell it well: Communicating the gospel across cultures*. Beacon Hill.

Severson, B. (2020). *Not done yet: Reaching and keeping unchurched emerging adults*. InterVarsity Press.

Smith, J. K. A. (2016). *You are what you love: The spiritual power of habit*. Brazos.

About the Author

Dr. W. Jay Moon, Professor of Evangelism & Church Planting and Director of the Office of Faith, Work, and Economics at Asbury Theological Seminary, served 13 years as a missionary with SIM, largely in Ghana, West Africa, among the Builsa people focusing on church planting and water development. He is the president of the Great Commission Research Network (GCRN) and the Association of Professors of Mission (APM).

GREAT COMMISSION
RESEARCH JOURNAL
2022, Vol. 14(2) 133-136

My Journey in Church Growth

Elmer Towns
Liberty University

I was first challenged with church growth in 1952 when I was a pastor of Westminster Presbyterian Chapel, Savannah, Georgia, and a student at Columbia Bible College, Columbia, South Carolina. The little Presbyterian mission chapel had five ladies conducting a Sunday school for approximately eight children. I became their pastor and led the church to grow to approximately 60 people. I had a burden to grow the church and I felt God could do it, but I had no knowledge of how to do it, and I had never seen or experienced church growth.

Later as a student at Dallas Theological Seminary, I pastored a chapel of the Scofield Memorial Church, which was famous for its former pastor Dr. C. I. Scofield, editor of the Scofield Reference Bible, and was known for its Bible teaching ministry, not church growth or evangelism. The church consisted of around 25 people meeting in West Dallas, considered a poverty-stricken area near downtown Dallas. The neighborhood had approximately 50 two-bedroom homes cheaply built without indoor plumbing (but with outhouses), reflecting the low socio-economic condition of the neighborhood. Again, I wanted this church to grow and did all I could to reach the neighborhood. Each year I knocked on every door in that neighborhood explaining the gospel trying to get people to church. While there, we were able to construct four Sunday school classrooms and bathrooms for both men and women. On a few occasions, attendance was over 100.

While in Dallas I became a friend of W. A. Criswell, pastor of First Baptist Church. He introduced me to the laws of Sunday school growth, well-known in the Southern Baptist Convention as the organizational foundation for evangelism and growth. Dr. Criswell had one of the largest attended churches in America.

The Ten Largest Sunday Schools

Out of that positive experience with Dr. Criswell against a personal background of little church growth, I wrote an article on the laws of Sunday school growth that was published in the *National Sunday School Association Encyclopedia*. That article also included spiritual motivations for church growth; outreach was not just organizational adjustments. It is then I began to research and published *The Ten Largest Sunday Schools* (Baker Book House, 1969), which identified large, fast-growing churches across the United States. The book captured the attention of the evangelical world and stayed on the Christian bestsellers list for seven months in 1970.

One of the churches in that book was Thomas Road Baptist Church, pastored by Jerry Falwell, Sr., who had planted that church in his hometown of Lynchburg, Virginia. It had grown from a handful of people to over 2,700 in attendance.

Because of our friendship and that book, Falwell invited me to co-found Liberty University with him in 1971. Our passion was to train young champions for Christ who would go out to plant great soul-winning churches, just as Jerry had done, and saturate their hometowns with the gospel to reach the entire population for Jesus Christ.

The church growth movement of the college led me to publish, *Capturing Your Town for Christ* (Jerry Falwell and Elmer Towns, Fleming Revell, 1973). Again, the book hit the bestselling list and sold over 100,000 copies.

Beginning in the early 1970s I researched and listed the 100 largest Sunday schools in America on the pages of *Christian Life Magazine* for which I was the Sunday School editor. Robert Walker, the editor of the magazine, said that news of the largest Sunday schools in America hit the nation like a lightning bolt and motivated thousands of pastors and leaders to build churches as large as these churches.

Praise/Worship Churches

Twenty years later, in the early 1990s, churches were growing but not through Sunday school outreach. The dynamic ministry of the pastors, combined with the energizing worship music in the morning services reflected energy...optimism...and demonstrated the presence of God. I found churches without Sunday school growing, most of them built on small groups or home Bible studies. In 1991, I published *Ten of Today's Most Innovative Churches* (Destiny Image Publishers), telling the story of megachurches across America reaching thousands each week.

Dynamic church growth moved away from organized Sunday school outreach to the drawing power of worship music in the auditorium. In its early days, I interviewed a middle-aged church-attending father who said, "Church was never exciting to me." Then he explained how his life was transformed, "I walked into a different church; the men there did not have ties on, and I felt a little overdressed. Then I heard the beat of the drums and the sound of the electric guitars. As soon as I reached my seat, I joined in singing the words I saw on the screen ... music I had never heard, and words that I did not know. The excitement of worship captured my heart. My hands went up in worship as tears trickled down from my eyes. The praise/worship environment captured my heart ... but most of all I found Jesus as my Savior."

A new generation – the Baby Boomer generation – did music in a new and different way, transforming the way Christians did worship. For over 400 years Protestant Christians had sung music like Martin Luther and the reformers. They had listened to sermons like those preached by John Calvin and John Wesley. That which was transforming everything was...Jesus!

Bill Hybels, in the greater Chicago suburb of Barrington, had attendance averaging over 20,000 weekly in multiple worship services. Not to be outdone, Rick Warren planted the Saddleback Church south of Los Angeles in Orange County, running over 25,000 worshipers weekly.

The music was about Jesus who became real to the worshipers. The preaching was about Jesus; again, He became real to the listeners. When worshipers were focused on Jesus, lives were transformed. Jesus was the "drawing power" for these new growing churches.

The Multisite Church Movement

In 2020, I published *Ten of the Largest Church Ministries Aggressively Touching the World* (Destiny Image Publishers). This new transformation in the church growth movement was ushered in by the power of transportation and the Internet. The ubiquity of the automobile, plus airplanes and other means of mass transportation, opened up the world to travel. This new freedom permitted Christianity to *carry* its worship of Jesus from one home church to many other church sites. Thus, the multisite church was born.

But more than transportation, there was an explosion of communication. Advances in computer networking led to the *World Wide*

Web, and with it came instant communication of text and images. Next, came instant multimedia communication. A mother church could capture their dynamic worship on a small camera and instantly communicate their worship excitement to other church locations. As a result, one local church with multiple congregations around the world can worship together. When people in one part of the world see and experience others in another part of the world lifting hands in worship, they share in the joy and enthusiasm together.

Congregations are no longer confined to a single building, whether large or small. The life-changing worship experience within the mother church is instantly communicated to daughter churches across town, across state lines, or around the world.

The multisite church has become the new means to carry the gospel around the world, doing it with multiple services in multiple locations. The prime example today is Hillsong Church in Australia with over 12,000 in attendance in its home sanctuary but reaching many national capitals around the world with worship services connected by the Internet. Christians in London, New York, Los Angeles, Suva (Fiji), Seoul, and dozens of other locations are worshiping together, almost a quarter of a million worshipers every Sunday.

GREAT COMMISSION
RESEARCH JOURNAL
2022, Vol. 14(2) 137-140

Book Review

Apostolic Imagination: Recovering a Biblical Vision for the Church's Mission Today

By J. D. Payne
Grand Rapids: Baker Academic, 2022
224 pages
$22.99

Reviewed by: Rev. Dr. H. L. "Scooter" Ward, Jr. Scooter serves as associate pastor and minister of music to Community Church in Santa Rosa Beach, FL. After earning his B.A. in Theology from Southeastern Bible College in Birmingham, AL, he was commissioned as an officer in the United States Air Force. He holds an M.A. in Christian Studies and an M.Div. from Luther Rice Seminary in Lithonia, GA, and a Doctor of Worship Studies from Liberty University in Lynchburg, VA.

It is not what you think. The phrase began quite differently. It was a simple, yet funny statement: "I am a ladybug rowing a lettuce boat with oars made from baby spoons." After being relayed several times by whispering from one person to the next, it ended up being completely altered: "A Miami lady grows a lot of oats on her farm to make baby food." It commonly happens when this well-known children's game is played. The telephone game involves several people that relay an initial message by whispering down the line of players, one at a time until the message reaches the last person. Each time the message is passed, it can easily be miscommunicated in the relay process or misunderstood by the recipient who discerns it. The more people involved in relaying it, the more potential for error exists. The message becomes completely changed in transmission. This illustrates what author J. D. Payne believes has happened in relation to missions in the Church. The first-century examples of missions in both belief and practice far differ from what the contemporary Church believes and practices as missions. Payne highlights the need to re-evaluate missions considering the first century examples from the early Church in the New Testament Scriptures.

Tenured pastor and professor of Christian ministry at Samford University, J. D. Payne has spent over nineteen years training students for ministry. In his most recent book, *Apostolic Imagination*, Payne outlines his desire for the Church to recover a biblical vision regarding its mission. He writes:

> When the Church is unwilling to return to the Scriptures in constant evaluation and reformation for both doctrine and practice, then the Church has revealed a most pathetic stewardship. Such a Church may be a hearer and a doer of the Word, but the doing is limited to the letter of the law of tradition and not the Spirit of mission. The weightier matters have been neglected as five billion people remain outside the body of Christ. (7)

Payne encourages an apostolic imagination that is biblically based, but adaptable to context in practice. He defines apostolic imagination as "a Spirit-transformed mindset" that helps to "facilitate urgent and widespread gospel proclamation, disciple making, church planting, and leadership development" (12). It is "connected to history and present reality" and "it demands returning to the first century and asking questions related to both belief and practice" (13). It is "an attempt to understand the imagination that the Spirit and the Word created and shaped, which resulted in the multiplication of disciples, churches, and leaders" (5). Payne clarifies that apostolic imagination is not equivalent to apostolic succession: "No one may claim the original apostolic office and authority. The apostolic imagination applied today is much different from the first-century apostles in this area...authority today comes from one's relationship with Christ and his Word *already* revealed" (68).

Payne also clarifies the importance of contextualization: "While the Church can and should learn from the New Testament (somehow), the Church's context is king for understanding language and definitions. The first century is unlike the fifth, fifteenth, or twenty-first; therefore, mission understanding and practice will evolve" (32). "Every generation must continually return to the Scriptures to make certain they are aligning themselves with 'the faith that was once for all delivered to the saints' (Jude 3)" (5). The apostolic element of the Christian faith is indispensable; however, belief and practice must be continually reformed by the Spirit of

God and the Word of God.

Payne believes "the Church has become lost in the disciple-making task" and "ventured away from the apostolic path and continues down a road involving numerous important and good activities labeled as missions" (4). He explains this drift away from an apostolic model "has greatly hindered the dissemination of the gospel across the world" as "missionaries became less involved in cross-cultural evangelism and church planting and more engaged with Christians" (38-39). A pastoral model has supplanted the apostolic model found in the examples of Jesus and the apostles from the first century. "The greatest need for evangelism today is intercultural evangelistic labors, both across the street and across the world" (42). Payne distinguishes the pastoral versus the apostolic in this way:

> The apostolic mindset and pastoral mindset operate two different paradigms of ministry, which do not need to be mutually exclusive...The mind of the pastor is on the established church. Such ministry is complex in nature. The apostolic imagination has a pastoral bent but operates initially in the context with no believers, no churches, no structures. Such ministry is simple in nature and consists primarily of basic tasks. The apostolic imagination sees ministry with one church as temporal and with planned role changes. Strategy is developed to begin the ministry with the end in mind and for contextualized leaders to become overseers. (183)

Payne highlights the importance of pastoral roles as necessary to sustain church growth, mission work, and edify the churches that are planted by apostolic teams. He clarifies, "Pastors are to be permanent fixtures with churches; apostolic teams are to be scaffolds until the work is complete" (39). Payne also reveals that "few pastors have developed apostolic imagination...Many may have the conviction of reaching the nations, are able to preach on the topic, and know that global disciple making is important, but lack apostolic experience" (182).

A reformation of strategy to prioritize and properly steward resources for missions will ensure that "the biblical understanding of the apostolic work is primarily about crossing cultural gaps, not oceans...The geographic boundaries outlined in Acts 1:8 have more to do with cultural differences than geographical distances" (148-149). "While local churches are to engage in a variety of ministries at home and abroad, a Great Commission triage should be in place. Mission involves multiple tasks, but the Church's apostolic work is to be given first order" (114).

This book is a great resource for pastors, elders, and missionaries to help clarify biblical responsibilities and priorities in mission endeavors. It will serve to help churches clarify the role of missions in the life of the Church and help local churches better steward their resources in fulfilling the Great Commission. Payne is very articulate in his dealing with the topic of missions. His passion for setting the Church back on track in its mission work is driven by the growing number of lost souls (over 4.5 billion by recent estimate) that need to hear the Gospel message (152). He writes:

A failure to communicate clearly and biblically, when it comes to the apostolic work of the Church, reveals a significant problem in stewarding well the Lord's commission...If the Lord has assigned a task to the Church, then it is necessary to have a clear understanding regarding the task and the Lord's expectations. The apostolic imagination strives for a clarity of understanding, for much is at stake before his return. (83-84)

Payne's passion is contagious, and this book helps facilitate action steps for churches to follow in reframing mission philosophy and practice in a way that clearly and accurately models what the early Church experienced. He supports the need for stewardship of mission resources under the guidance of the Holy Spirit to sustain disciple-making efforts both locally and globally. Payne defines success as "recognized more as faithfulness to calling and the Lord's leadership and as stewardship of opportunities and resources in view of the Church's task and global realities" (162-163). The book concludes with a special section written to help pastors navigate the next steps. Pastors will find this resource quite beneficial in their efforts to revitalize and mobilize their respective churches to carry out the Great Commission more effectively.

GREAT COMMISSION
RESEARCH JOURNAL
2022, Vol. 14(2) 141-146

Book Review

Advanced Missiology: How to Study Missions in Credible and Useful Ways

By Kenneth R. Nehrbass
Eugene, OR, Cascade Books, 2021
337 pages
USD $30.40, Paperback

Reviewed by Keith R. Sellers. Keith has served with WorldVenture Mission in Hungary for over 21 years. He has a B.A. in Christian Missions, an M.A. in Bible, and an M.Div. from Bob Jones University as well as a D.Min. in Growing and Multiplying Churches from Biola University. His ministry experiences include evangelism, church planting and revitalization, and TCK education.

The text is explicitly a critical exploration of foundational missiology as its main title suggests. On the other hand, the subtitle expresses the instrumental nature of the text, "How to Study Missions in Credible and Useful Ways." The very title presents a frustrating tension in this often-misunderstood field of knowledge: It is practical and very complex at the same time. Nehrbass suggests a couple of introductory texts for the uninitiated and those who may have studied it in a previous decade (7). Using the phrase "cross-cultural discipleship" as a definition for missions, he guides the reader down the grand river of missiology highlighting its numerous tributaries as well as its key intellectual and spiritual dangers. This study should attract scholars and thoughtful practitioners alike since both may sometimes encounter dead ends in the confusing labyrinth of missiological opinions. Because an advanced exploration of the river of missiology requires the use of many disciplines, Nehrbass wisely collaborated with other scholars. Rebeca de la Torre Burnett, Leanne

Dzubinski, and Julie Martinez made valuable contributions to the book (chapters 6, 7, and the missiologist profiles). The short profiles of the field's most prominent thinkers provide both personal inspiration and historical perspective.

In the first chapter, Nehrbass strives for a consistent definition of missiology without falling into the extremes of excessively limiting it, nor making it too broad to include everything. He highlights the extremely multidisciplinary nature of crossing cultures and making disciples. Recognizing the limits of the old "three-legged stool" metaphor, he proposes the image of a dynamic river to help us better understand missiology (7, 16, 27-30). The author provides the following definition of missiology: "The use of academic disciplines to bring the church across cultural boundaries for the sake of making disciples" (18). This thoughtful and practical definition guides the book's discussion of how specific disciplines relate to the task of making disciples in other cultures.

In chapter two, "Connecting Theology to Cross-Cultural Discipleship," Nehrbass explores a viable path toward comprehending the relationships between theology and mission. Although missiology began as a subfield under schools of theology in which theologians would develop a "theology of missions" (38), missionary efforts at making disciples have historically driven the discussion of theology so that theologians and practitioners can better explain Christianity to other ethno-linguistic groups. Nehrbass offers what he calls a "systematic missiological theology" as an alternative to the "mission of God" and "missions is everywhere" views (43-44). He makes a distinction between a "missional hermeneutic" and what he calls a "missiological hermeneutic." Nehrbass claims that his "missiological hermeneutic" specifically focuses on the idea of cross-cultural discipleship and includes the *missio Dei* theology's broad view of God's missional plan to redeem humanity. Some readers may see this critique and added terminology as unnecessary since they already wed *missio Dei* theology with the Great Commission.

Chapter three shows how missiologists use history to conduct better research for best practices in the present. The author provides six lenses for understanding the history of missions or the expansion of Christianity (76). The fifth and sixth approaches, "emphasizing specific strategies of missions" and "building missiological theory," are perhaps the most beneficial lenses for practitioners. For scholars of missiological history, he provides practical examples of topics to research (78).

Chapter four addresses the controversial field of anthropology and the complicated love-hate relationship missiologists have with it. While Christian scholars disdain the extreme cultural relativism and antireligious rationalism of secular anthropology, the text makes a strong case for engaging with it. Because Christians desire to bring every aspect of culture under the lordship of Christ, they must understand the cultural spheres of His dominion. Anthropology helps us better understand those cultural spheres. The chapter refutes past criticisms that anthropologists made against missionaries, and it notes how postmodernism pushed anthropology to a more inclusive stance. The author describes the dynamic tension between empowering culture and changing it to the point of committing what critics call ethnocide (110). Theologically minded readers might observe that the tension exists because we as bearers of God's image create culture, and at the same time we are fallen creatures whose cultural norms need transformation.

Closely related to anthropology, chapter five addresses the nebulous concept of intercultural studies, which Nehrbass defines as "the academic field that examines the experiences of people who cross cultural boundaries" (140). This chapter helps cross-cultural workers uncover ethnocentric attitudes and simplistic stereotypes. The three main branches of this discipline include intercultural communication, intercultural adjustment, and intercultural leadership. The chapter addresses the specific dynamics which may lead to very thorny situations when Westerners engage other cultures. These dynamics are playing out in North American churches as the older generation embraces individualism and status quo while the emerging generations tend to prefer collectivism and innovation. Churches in multicultural communities with many new immigrants should pay attention to the descriptions of how newcomers may acculturate (149). The description of what constitutes a healthy cultural intelligence is quite liberating for the expat practitioner (151).

In chapter six Martinez and Nehrbass connect development theories to cross-cultural discipleship. Their logical and theological argument for development ministry flows from the cultural mandate (Gen 1:28) to Christ's great commands about loving God and others. They claim that development is about restoring broken relationships with God, government, society, land, and people (156). Mending these relationships helps people to become better disciples. The chapter traces the holism-prioritism debate up to the Lausanne Committee's influential resolution that social action follows, precedes, and accompanies evangelism (161). The reader will learn about the most significant theories of community development and suggested venues of empirical research.

Connecting education to cross-cultural discipleship in chapter seven, Burnett and Dzubinski address formal (schools) and non-formal (in churches) educational approaches concerning their effectiveness, contextualization, outcomes, and preparation. Other missiology texts usually ignore cross-cultural education, but it has been a valuable tool among missionaries for the past two hundred years. Of special note for missionary educators, formal educational approaches must be holistic, locally contextualized, experiential, and inclusive to be effective (182-83, 189). Unfortunately, evangelical churches have become too preoccupied with financing overseas church planting initiatives to the neglect of this extremely valuable tool of making disciples and anchoring new generations with a Christian worldview. Churches and agencies might consider developing missionary teams that integrate both education and church planting. Very recent surges of immigration and diaspora due to the wars in Syria and Ukraine have produced dire educational needs among immigrant children, whose parents may readily welcome bilingual Christian schools. Perhaps bilingual Christian schools, or programs that address the needs of third culture kids, may address needs for immigrants coming across US borders. Churches attempting to reach immigrant adults who are "low-literate" should consider using more oral communication methods which contribute to both their learning of the Bible and English (193).

Defining cross-cultural discipleship, chapter eight begins the second section of the book, "The Distributaries of Missiology." Nehrbass asserts that the Great Commission is the "*sine qua non* of missiology," and he shows how theory connects with practice (199). Because the concept of cross-cultural discipleship is an integral part of the book, some readers may prefer a definition in the beginning, but its presentation here unveils an interesting climax to the overall flow. This chapter deals with two particularly fuzzy, yet crucial words: disciple and missionary. The ancient word disciple proves difficult to nail down since it originates outside of the Western educational context. The author describes a missionary as "someone who is sent by a Christian community primarily for the purpose of making disciples across cultures" (206). He leaves it up to the reader to decide whether specific fuzzy examples of workers belong to the category of "missionary" (206-08).

Chapters nine and ten describe seminal theories and models in missiology. Chapter nine reviews key theories that shaped missiology and encourages readers to explore new ways of understanding the gospel's effective dissemination. He lists strengths and weaknesses of well-known theories. The text leans in favor of the Homogenous Unit theory, which provides a valuable starting point to reach a specific people (219), who eventually should become more heterogeneous (Gal 2:28). Chapter ten surveys the most popular models that have influenced missiological theory and practice. To both the uninitiated and well-read, missiology's historic usage of the term "model" remains a source of frustration since it does not denote a complex methodological scheme, but it merely provides a launching point into the grand river of missiology. Nehrbass speaks highly of the Three Selves Model, which strives for indigeneity and independence, but then he questions its goal of self-determination and proposes that churches should instead become interdependent (238).

Chapter eleven provides a view to the latest trends and possible directions in the future of missiology. Nehrbass justifiably warns about the need to rethink closure theology, and he provides an action list to make missiology a more useful discipline (301). Missiology will continue to become more influenced by women scholars and researchers from non-Western contexts.

Nehrbass has studied hundreds of missiological texts from multiple disciplines to produce this valuable work. The book's panoramic view of the broad river of missiology helps the practitioner visualize where he or she has already traversed. Because the book contains numerous analyses of the pros and cons of various theories and models, practitioners and theorists may find themselves both offended and affirmed. The text indirectly comprises a veritable list of dialectical tensions that exist in carrying out the Great Commission. Those looking for easy answers and an easy read will be unfulfilled. The book serves as a catalyst for missiological research and hands-on experimentation in doing mission. It should compel readers to re-examine their views on critical issues related to missiology.

Perhaps the multiple dilemmas in the text arise from the fact that most missiologists have originated in the West where there exists a robust propensity to atomize, categorize, and form propositions that apply in every context. A few dialectical tensions mentioned throughout the text include empowering culture vs. ethnocide (110), Andrew Wall's poles of indigenizing vs. a supra-cultural pilgrim principle (210), McGavran's homogeneous unit vs. a heterogenous church (219), Winter's modality/sodality model (224), Pike's emic and etic distinctions of cultural analysis (226), ethno-theology vs. a supra-cultural kernel (244), indiscriminate sowing vs. one-time strategic sowing of the gospel (251), and heart language vs. language of wider communication (268).

Missiology's dilemmas may be largely rooted in contemporary epistemological dilemmas relating to the confluence of modernity with post modernity. The text reveals that some scholars tended to follow a faulty either-or thinking or the logical fallacy of a false dilemma. Scholars and practitioners must seek a coherency and harmony rising not only from empirical research, but also from Scriptural examples of contextualization (242), practical wisdom, and cross-cultural collaboration among Spirit-led leaders (245).

As globalization continues and Christianity declines in the West, church planters, pastors, evangelists, educators, and missionaries must become better versed in missiology. Christian leaders must improve their integration of missiology and theology. Churches, mission agencies, and theological schools cannot remain disconnected from each other, but they must synthesize their resources, energies, and knowledge in order to fulfill the Great Commission. *Advanced Missiology* will help these institutions to engage and challenge the world to obey all that Christ commanded.

GREAT COMMISSION
RESEARCH JOURNAL
2022, Vol. 14(2) 147-149

Book Review

Cultural intelligence: Living for God in a Diverse, Pluralistic World

By Darrell Bock
Nashville, TN: B&H Academic, 2020
128 pages
USD $19.99, Paperback

Reviewed by Kenneth Nehrbass. Kenneth Nehrbass, Ph.D., is an anthropology and translation consultant with the Summer Institute of Linguistics and is the Director of Special Projects at California Baptist University.

  Cultural Intelligence is a short, popular-level text about sharing the Christian faith in an increasingly secular world. Despite the title's resemblance to the theories of cultural intelligence (CQ), the text does not interact with the CQ model that has been popularized in missiology. However, the text does cover a question that is core to missiology: How can we share the good news with the wider culture? By "culture" Bock has in mind the majority culture found within the USA, which is becoming increasingly at odds with the Christian subculture. In fact, Bock suggests that (Western?) culture (he does not explicitly name *which* culture) is closer to the paganism of the Roman empire than to the Christianity of Western Europe in previous centuries: Our neighbors may not believe in truth, and may not have absolute moral standards.

  Bock explains that to be culturally intelligent in this glocalized, secular context means understanding the values, customs and social institutions of agnostics and atheists. And to challenge those values and customs, we must be mindful of the ways we engage secular folks in conversations about religious ideas. He draws on some key scriptures that should inform such conversations. For example, his exegesis of Ephesians 6:10-18 reminds us that we are engaged in a spiritual battle. And Bock urges us to read off of 1 Peter 3:13-18, rather than stopping at verse 15 (be ready with a defense). We must *also* read the part about having gentleness and respect.

A recurring thesis in the book is that the gospel is both an invitation and a challenge (38). This invitation/challenge motif is an "enormous tension" (97) throughout the New Testament and for anyone who wants to be salt and light: On the one hand, the gospel is good news; on the other hand, the evangelist must share the bad news of how our culture has rebelled, so people will see why the good news is, in fact, good. To develop this invitation/challenge concept, Bock juxtaposes Paul's *theology* of evangelism in Romans 1 (e.g. "all are without excuse") to his *methodology* of evangelism in Acts 17 (e.g. Paul referred to the Athenians' own cultural texts, and offered them hope) (52).

The book draws on communication theory to show how our messages are multi-layered. Bock refers to the triphonic (three-sound) nature of communication (54): 1) the *content* (Bock refers to this as the "facts"); 2) the *filters* (our emotions and perceptions); and 3) our *identity* (this can include our goals for communication, and the relationship between the conversation partners). Bock's advice is that we use our awareness of these three layers to become better listeners. Our goal should be to understand, not just to win an argument.

The text contains some heuristic devices: One scale helps the reader to determine the level of conviction he or she holds regarding a particular issue. Another checklist helps the reader determine the extent to which an issue matters in the eternal scope of things. These tools can help evangelists "major on the majors" (this is not Bock's term).

To develop a theology of cultural engagement, Bock spends some time on the relationship between the Creation Mandate and the Great Commission. He exhorts us that "salvation is about more than the cross" (79). Discipleship involves learning how to carry out the creation mandate in ways that honor God and others, so we can "manage our world and its relationships well" (82).

Toward the end, Bock lays out a suggested course-correction for the way the church handles the ministry of proclamation. He affirms that (evangelical) churches are typically good at reading the "Bible to life" (105). That is, they exegete a passage and apply it to a situation. But Bock suggests that we should become more skilled at reading "life to the Bible" (106). This is more challenging, because it requires that we become aware of contemporary trends in the culture, and show, with grace and hope, what the Bible has to say about those issues. But Bock warns that we should stop focusing on a few pet social and theological issues which make the church seem irrelevant to so many people. Instead, our message must have many intersections with the daily lives of secular people, as Abraham Kuyper tried to do (96). Specific examples of such cultural issues include racial identity, wealth, work, guns, world religions, and immigration. Bock supplies some scriptural passages for examining each of these issues.

Because of its brevity, *Cultural Intelligence* does not delve into rich examples of how secular people have come to faith through the methods that Bock suggests. But the book supplies ample scriptural support (and cultural insight) for the approaches that are developed throughout the text.

GREAT COMMISSION
RESEARCH JOURNAL
2022, Vol. 14(2) 151-154

Book Review

Development in Mission: A Guide for Transforming Global Poverty and Ourselves

By Monty Lynn, Rob Gailey, and Derran Reese
Abilene Christian University Press, 2021
269 pages
US$20.99

Reviewed by Nathaniel (Than) Veltman, who currently serves as Mission Scholar in Missiology and Community Development with United World Mission's Theological Education Initiative at the Ethiopian Graduate School of Theology in Addis Ababa, Ethiopia.

What makes development *transformational*? And does transformation include the giver as much as the receiver? Distilling insights to answer these questions is the focus of *Development in Mission*. In this collaborative work by Monty Lynn, Rob Gailey, and Derran Reese, readers are presented with "fresh perspectives on holistic mission and transformational development" (28). The end goal is a contribution to the transformation of missionaries, relief and development workers, congregations and individuals, primarily from the Global North, who aspire to alleviate global poverty. Principles and practices rooted in a biblical understanding of holistic mission are offered as a guide for those seeking to engage transformational development around the world.

The book consists of three parts. Part One focuses on "deepening understanding" of mission and transformational development. In Chapter 1, the authors issue a call to balance the blessing of giving and receiving, acknowledging that historically the poor are limited to the receiving end. Instead, the rich should not "keep all of the blessings [of giving] for

[them]selves" (25) and learn to both experience the blessings of receiving while simultaneously allowing others to experience the blessing of giving. This is followed in Chapter 2 by an examination of holistic mission and *missio Dei*. The authors note that the mission of God extends to all of creation, and they highlight the central role of Christ's work of salvation. They also present an argument for including poverty alleviation in holistic mission. Part 1 concludes in Chapter 3 with a consideration of "what is unique, if anything, about *Christian* efforts to care for vulnerable populations and mitigate poverty" (64). The authors suggest that the end of Christian transformational development is God and the means of getting there is the "way of Jesus" (71-75). Such a pursuit is grounded in seven principles to guide congregations: cultivating loving relationships; empowering to sustain; giving it time; attending to context; investing in friendships and partnerships; seeking out insight; and assessing and improving (76-92).

Part Two is one chapter and the longest in the book at 83 pages. The focus here shifts to examining transformational development sectors. For each sector, the authors "offer an introduction, including theological warrant for some less-known sectors, along with research- and field-based insights and practices" (95). Discussion includes well-known development sectors such as education, food, health, and water, sanitation and hygiene as well as less-known sectors of freedom and liberation, sport, technology, and others. Readers may be surprised to read about scripture translation and relief. Engagement with each sector is primarily descriptive, but the authors point readers to additional resources in Appendix B that provides lists of organizations working in each sector.

Part Three consists of two chapters focused on "moving forward." Chapter 5 focuses on tools and processes for engagement with transformational development at the congregational level (including potential subgroups contained within churches, such as mission boards and ministry teams). As the authors note, "the steps outlined...are intended to be not a formula for success but, instead, suggested mindsets and practices that will help churches discern and engage faithfully while also maturing as disciples and co-laborers in God's mission in the world" (183). They begin with prayer and self-reflection, recognizing the spiritual nature of such engagement. This is followed by tools for discernment, including mental models of poverty and development (189-191), and it ends with a discussion of the transformational nature of development (207-209). Part Three concludes in Chapter 6 with an eye to "looking ahead"- recognizing the world today has changed significantly with global shifts in religion and the broader field of development itself.

Taken together, this book addresses an important need: providing congregations, and individuals, with a resource for engaging the broad and diverse field of international development. The authors rightly note that "[c]ongregations or individuals wanting to engage in global mission have much to consider and a multitude of available paths. The task ahead can leave us unsure of how to take a step forward" (182). Indeed, the field of transformational development can be overwhelming, perhaps explaining the many observed shortcomings of much international engagement efforts by congregations in the Global North as they rush to enter the fray of poverty alleviation. The remedy presented in this book is to slow down, consider individual and congregational gifts and skills, and embody a process that transforms both the giver and receiver. Perhaps most significantly, the book does not ignore the spiritual dynamics of mission and transformational development, giving brief attention to transformational liturgies (207). Although much of the book addresses congregations, individuals would benefit from this book as well.

Although a helpful guide, there are two critiques that stand out. First, the authors pack in a lot of description in the chapter on development sectors. This is perhaps inevitable given the broad range of development work, but this limits the authors to description, and it elides an in-depth examination of each sector from the perspective of holistic mission. Readers may feel inclined to skip to sections deemed relevant to them, as the authors note, but the overall result is a rather quick overview. As an introduction to the basic names, focus and practices of various development sectors, this book hits the mark. Readers will need to look elsewhere for deeper engagement with particular development sectors. Secondly, discussion of some development sectors requires more nuance. A discussion of disabilities under the health sector, for example, ignores important distinctions highlighted in recent research in disabilities studies. This book unnecessarily embraces a medical model of disability without giving sufficient attention to the need for addressing the social model of disability, which requires deeper social transformation. Similarly, including relief and humanitarian aid under the broad scope of development ignores fundamental differences between relief and development. Finally, the sector of scripture translation lacks necessary warrant for inclusion as a development sector beyond the observation that "an encounter with God in Scripture can enhance flourishing in multiple areas of life" (164). This is true in any context; left unexplored are questions of what is the explicit connection to transformational development and what specific encounters might occur in the process engaging the transformational development process?

With an overall aim of distilling what makes development *transformational* and how both the giver and receiver are transformed, this book achieves its goal. Teachers and church leaders seeking to provide a basic introduction to transformational development in mission will find in this book a useful resource. Deep engagement with the principles and practices outlined will contribute to greater human flourishing and *shalom* for those in the Global North and the Global South.

GREAT COMMISSION

RESEARCH JOURNAL

2022, Vol. 14(2) 155-159

Book Review

Pastor Unique: Becoming a Turnaround Leader

By Lavern E. Brown, Gordon E. Penfold, and Gary J. Westra
WestBow Press, 2016
354 pages
$24.95

Reviewed by Jim Roden. He has a passion for church revitalization and is currently the lead pastor at The Journey Church in Tucson, Arizona. He recently defended his doctoral dissertation at Talbot School of Theology in completion of his Doctorate of Ministry degree. He earned his M.Div. from Western Seminary and B.A. from The Master's University.

It is no secret that churches in North America are struggling in their God-given mission to make disciples for Jesus Christ. Yet we are in a post-Christian culture, and many churches are stagnant or in decline. Only 15 to 20 percent of all evangelical churches in North America are growing and only a portion of these are growing through the conversion and addition of lost souls to faith in Jesus Christ. This is a time and place that calls for bold leadership, sacrificial effort, fervent prayer, and solid research of best practices in the area of church revitalization.

Pastor Unique, written by Lavern Brown, Gordon Penfold, and Gary Westra, is a well-researched book that focuses on what is required to effectively lead church revitalization in the midst of this challenging cultural context. Brown, Penfold, and Westra met online because of their common passion for local church revitalization. *Pastor Unique* is the fruit of their friendship and collaborative efforts. All three have individually earned a place at the table through years of pastoral ministry as well as their personal interest in church leadership best practices through careful and thorough research. *Pastor Unique* is written for pastors, church leaders, and denominational executives who want to understand which leadership behaviors promote church renewal and which behaviors hinder it as well as how to apply these behaviors in order to realize revitalization so they can effectively minister in the local church. While it is written as a one stop, do-it-all book on church revitalization, its greatest contribution is the discovery of statistically significant differences between naturally hardwired turnaround pastors called "TAPs" and those who are not naturally hardwired as turnaround pastors called "NTAPs."

Pastor Unique is written for a very clear purpose. In the introduction, the authors develop a sense of urgency for the subject matter at hand. The reader is left with a sense of anticipation for the rest of the book's content. Chapters one through three introduce what the authors perceive to be the need for assessment–based training and coaching beyond basic seminary training as well as the primary factors that they believe contribute to ineffectiveness in churches and church leadership. In this section, the authors also address the need for pastors to see themselves the way God sees them. They attempt to help readers understand and begin to believe that they are called and gifted by God to accomplish significant things for Jesus Christ through their pastoral ministries.

In chapters four and five, the authors take time to explain their research strategy and their preference for what is called the Birkman Method, which is a personality assessment tool. They explain why they believe this method is superior to other personality assessments. This is also where they reveal their discoveries of what leadership behaviors distinguish TAPs from NTAPs.

In chapters six through eight, the authors lead the reader into the application of their research findings regarding best practices for leadership. This is where the authors develop their theology of spiritual leadership and explain why they believe that firm and directive leadership is essential for leading systemic change in the local church. They also begin to integrate their research with change-management theory and conflict-management theory.

Denominational leader and church consultant Paul Borden, who specifically writes to denominational executives and leaders, is the author of chapter 9. His main agenda is to convince denominational leaders of the value of assessment-based training and coaching as well as cluster-group participation. Borden gives practical guidance as to how to use this book in denominational work. Finally, in chapter ten, Brown, Penfold, and Westra give a strategy that pastors can use in order to move forward and begin to behave as TAPs along with some practical next steps.

It is my opinion that the guest chapter by Borden is a bit awkward and misplaced. I would also recommend that it be designated as an appendix instead of a main chapter. It is also my opinion that Appendix C, "Turnaround Pastors Must Stand Apart," actually be placed in the main content of this book as one of the main chapters instead of being an appendix.

The authors hope to demonstrate that there are in fact measurable, statistically significant differences between TAPs and NTAPs using the Birkman assessment tool. They also hope to demonstrate that by adopting turnaround leadership best practices, even non-turnaround pastors can be successful in leading church revitalization. It is my opinion that Brown, Penfold, and Westra do a fantastic job of not only demonstrating this as a real possibility but also leading pastors and denominational leaders toward a hopeful future as they provide next steps for facilitating effective church revitalization. They accomplish this in *Pastor Unique* through helpful and engaging content, crisp writing, and real-life examples in an optimistic tone. They also encourage pastors to engage in best practices such as mentorship, cluster groups, and attending a "Turnaround Pastor Boot Camp."

Much of the content of *Pastor Unique* overlaps with, and is supported by, preexisting church revitalization research and theory; but chapter five is truly unique and original. It is my opinion that chapter five is the heart and soul of this book and is the most significant contribution to the church-growth movement and to the body of church revitalization research. In this chapter, the authors present seven statistically significant differences between TAPs and NTAPs.

> The seven statistically significant differences identified by our research included three Usual Behaviors, two Needs, and two Interests between NTAPs and TAPs. We discovered three Usual Behaviors that were significant: Authority, Change, and Freedom. We also found two Needs: Freedom and Thought. Finally, our research found two Interests that were different between TAPs and NTAPs: Music and Social Service. (81)

As a Usual Behavior, Authority means that a person is more likely to not only speak his opinion but to assert that opinion in a group. TAPs scored almost twice as high in this as NTAPs. Another Usual Behavior distinction between TAPs and NTAPs is Change. This relational component assesses a person's ability to deal with shifting priorities, be flexible, and remain patient with interruptions. "TAPs relish variety in the unexpected. NTAPs like things in sequence, minimal interruption, and no surprises" (84).

Freedom actually showed up in two different dimensions as a distinction between TAPs and NTAPs: Usual Behavior as well as Need. What this means is that TAPs thrive on the unexpected and relish multitasking. "Because of their Freedom Usual Behavior, TAPs – who tend to be individualistic – initiate their own course. Their Freedom Need scores mean that they want freedom in action and thought. They push against control and traditionalism" (86). TAPs live free and expect others to allow them to live free.

One of the surprising discoveries was the difference that the authors discovered between TAPs and NTAPs in Thought Need. They initially assumed that TAPs would be quick and decisive in their decision making. What they discovered was just the opposite: TAPs need "white space" for complex decision making. They need time to think, evaluate, and consider the consequences of many different courses of action before pulling the trigger on significant decisions whereas NTAPs are more likely to make quick or even impulsive decisions. It is the authors' belief that NTAPs do this because they are uncomfortable with ambiguity and tend to make quick decisions in order to alleviate internal discomfort and organizational anxiety. TAPs on the other hand, have a higher tolerance for ambiguity and can more easily stand apart from organizational anxiety and pressure.

There were two statistically significant interests that distinguished TAPs from NTAPs: Music and Social Services. The authors' theory on music is that TAPs are auditory learners and in touch with the way things sound. This would be important both for the musical quality of a worship service as well as the sound of their own preaching style and presentation. "If the worship services do not move people and generate passion for the Lord, they will not invite their friends to their church" (95).

The final statistically significant difference between these two groups of pastors was in the area of Social Service; and while both TAPs and NTAPs scored significantly higher than the general population in their interest in caring for others, TAPs scored lower than NTAPs. "NTAPs like the 'hands-on' aspect of ministry...They have a very strong desire to meet the emotional needs of others. They thrive on close contact with people, to teach, counsel, and comfort. They love the caring side of pastoral ministry" (96). Perhaps the lower Social Service Interest score of TAPs allows them to have the time and emotional energy to work on other leadership behaviors that contribute more clearly to church revitalization.

The authors demonstrate a clear bias toward firm and directive pastoral leadership but this bias is supported by their solid research on TAPs and supported in their writing with clear biblical teaching.

Overall, this book was powerful for me. I've been through it more than once and have found the TAPs best practices described within its pages to be vitally important to my church and personal leadership.

This book makes a very important contribution to the field of biblical church growth and revitalization. The content is presented in a helpful and engaging manner. Furthermore, it is my opinion that every church planter, lead pastor, seminarian, church consultant, seminary professor, denominational leader, and elder board should read this book. The research findings and content are simply that important!

Book Review

Defending Shame: Its Formative Power in Paul's Letters

By Te-Li Lau
Baker Academic, 2020
$28.00

Reviewed by Yi-Sang Patrick Chan. Patrick is a Ph.D. candidate at the University of Aberdeen, and is general secretary for Campus Crusade for Christ in Hong Kong.

Since the 1980s, by building upon social anthropologists' works, biblical scholars have employed the framework of "honor and shame" to study the culture of the ancient Mediterranean region. The New Testament socio-scientific group has approached the concept of shame from cultural and anthropological models of honor-shame that consider the Apostle Paul's use of shame as a means for social control. However, Lau argues that these authors merely define "shame vis-à-vis honor and understanding both as social values," and they do "not focus on the shame experience, nor...understand shame as a moral emotion" (10). That is, the socio-scientific honor-shame model has explained how a community maintains social control, but it does not focus on how an individual such as Paul brings about moral reformation in his converts via the practice of psychology (9).

In light of this, in his book *Defending Shame*, Lau examines "Paul's use of shame for Christian formation within his Jewish and Greco-Roman context and compares it with various contemporary perspectives" (10). The book's purpose is to respond to today's culture that possesses a "deep antagonism to shame." Lau raises the question of how we should appropriate the use of shame. Does it have a particular positive value? (5)

To answer this, Lau surveys Paul's use of shame in various letters and stresses its pedagogical function. In contrast to Bruce Malina's conception of shame, which only focuses on its social impact, Lau considers shame a moral and social emotion. Also, another significant difference between the socio-scientific honor-shame model and Lau's is that Lau considers the positive impact of the emotion of shame, and he explores its ethical significance. In order to do that, by engaging with the modern idea of emotion from psychologist Aaron Ben-Ze'ev, Lau argues that "what is essential and constitutive of the emotional experience is the appraisal or evaluative component" (15). Then, in defining shame, Lau argues that "the constitutive element is negative self-evaluation, the awareness of being seen to fall short of some perceived standard or ideal. The presence of another may be the catalyst, but the evaluation constitutive of shame still depends on the self" (16). He further draws on the insights from modern psychology to differentiate shame from humiliation, embarrassment, and guilt in order to arrive at a more nuanced understanding of the emotion of shame. Based on the analysis with the comparative work of modern psychology, Lau builds on a taxonomy of shame that focuses on its different functions, including 1) the occurrent experience of shame, 2) dispositional shame, 3) retrospective shame, 4) prospective shame, 5) act of shaming. He then applies this taxonomy to various texts in Paul's letters and discerns the specific function of shame that Paul uses to shape the community's identity formation.

In the subsequent chapters of the book, Lau provides a detailed analysis of how shame's moral relevance is demonstrated in different ancient literatures. He has studied the notion of shame in Greco-Roman philosophical context (chapter 2) and Jewish literature (chapter 3). Lau also has provided an exegetical analysis of the use of shame in various Pauline letters (chapters 4-6). By doing this, Lau locates his study of Paul "within the moral psychology of [Paul's] day" and studies how Paul appealed to shame as a moral emotion to "internally to reform individual mind and conscience" (7)

One notable feature of his book is that Lau has differentiated two notions of shame, namely, "a rhetoric of shame that tears down and a rhetoric of shame that builds up" (184). Lau explains that the rhetoric of shame that tears down is the Greco-Roman rhetoric that aims at exalting oneself at the expense of others. The rhetoric of shame that builds up is to challenge the people to see their errors in light of the message of the cross. For example, in his exegesis of 1 Corinthians, Lau argues that in 4:14, Paul adopts the latter function of shame while disowning the former function. For Lau, Paul is shaming the Corinthian community, which functions as a "pedagogical tool to transform the mind of his readers into the mind of Christ" (164). In order to support his argument of shaming, Lau further argues that the construction "not to shame but to admonish" (οὐ...ἀλλά) does not imply that shaming and admonition are polar opposites. Lau argues that the construction can also mean "not so much...as" in the way that the first element "is not entirely negated but toned down" (111). Following his analysis of the Greek usage of the construction, Lau argues that Paul's purpose is to repudiate any function of shame that does not support the task of admonition. In this regard, Lau's article has enlarged scholars' understanding of the conception of shame, for which shame can be used positively to help change people's moral behavior.

To conclude, by building upon a modern psychological understanding of shame, Lau has broadened the concept of shame and has set his work radically different from Malina's honor-shame model, which merely defines shame vis-à-vis honor. It is also important to note that although Lau builds on the modern psychological understanding of shame, his study is not anachronistic. In fact, his understanding of shame aligns with the Greco-Roman philosophical theory of emotion. Lau has also offered a comprehensive study by focusing on the various texts in the Greco-Roman context, Jewish literature, and Pauline letters. His study does not merely focus on a few shame lexemes but on the larger concept of shame by considering various shame-related word groups.

GREAT COMMISSION
RESEARCH JOURNAL
2022, Vol. 14(2) 165-169

Book Review

Motus Dei: The Movement of God to Disciple the Nations

Edited by Warrick Farah, Foreword by David Garrison, Afterword by Alan Hirsch
Littleton, CO: William Carey Publishing, 2021
376 pages
USD $26.99

Reviewed by David H. Campbell. David has a PhD in Missiology from the New Orleans Baptist Theological Seminary. He has some experience working among Muslims in Indonesia and with Hindus and Buddhists in Nepal. He currently teaches Christian Mission courses at Grand Canyon University and World Religions with Liberty University.

In his groundbreaking book, *Motus Dei: The Movement of God to Disciple the Nations,* Warrick Farah, a missiologist and theological educator from the Middle East, and a team of scholars, practitioners, mission leaders, and movement catalysts from around the world have come together to describe and document the miraculous movement of God among the nations in which thousands of Muslims, Buddhists, and Hindus in many previously Unreached People Groups (UPGs) are coming to faith in Jesus Christ in the past thirty years. Farah writes in the introduction to his book, "We are talking about movements of the kingdom of God. Church planting movements. Disciple making movements. Movements in which King Jesus is made famous, and lives and communities are being transformed by the gospel. Ultimately, we are talking about the motus dei: Latin for the 'movement of God" (xiii).

But what does Farah mean by the term movement? Movements are not methods, but rather a passion for Jesus Christ in which disciples make disciples and movements are simply the result. Movements are the "phenomenon of small, rapidly reproducing communities of obedient Christ followers. These communities of Christ followers may look different than the churches with which we are familiar. Yet they are growing remarkably and are currently estimated to constitute about 1 percent of the world's population" (331).

Motus Dei is divided into five main sections and includes twenty-two chapters on movements: Part I-The Big Picture of Movements, Part II-Missional Theology of Movements, Part III-Movement Dynamics, Part IV-Case Studies, and Part V-Movement Leadership and Next Steps. In Part 1, Farah provides a theological, sociological, and practical overview of movements. Farah notes, "While it can be described in several ways, Christianity is by nature a movement" (2). Farah posits that if biblical faith is motus Dei by nature, then a careful missiological examination of contemporary movements needs to be made to examine and discern what things could be promoting and hindering movements in both the Global South and potentially in the Global North.

Chapter two provides observations over fifteen years of Disciple Making Movements (DMMs) from a non-western perspective. Samuel Kebreab, the Regional Coordinator for the Horn of Africa with the Movement for African National Initiative (MANI) writes:

> I first heard of Disciple Making Movements (DMMs) in 2006, while I was going through a disheartening season. I was serving our denomination as outreach coordinator in a church planting effort we had started among the Yoma [a pseudonym], an unreached people group in Southern Ethiopia. We had aimed to plant one hundred village churches in fifteen years. By 2006, our seventh year of engaging the people, we had planted only seven churches. I felt discouraged... While attending DMM training by David Watson and David Hunt, I felt the material made a lot of sense. (26)

After his training in DMM, Kebreab began to train and coach Yoma men and women using DMM principles. The work grew slowly at first but steadily. After fourteen years, Kebreab joyfully reported, "There are now 5,672 Christ followers in 364 village churches, comprising seven generations of churches" (26). What happened? A DMM was initiated by God working among and through His people.

In chapter three, David Coles answers some of the critiques of movements and movement strategies. Coles deals with the eight most common objections to movements. One such objection he addresses is the charge that "Church Planting Movements leave open a door for false teaching because of inadequate theological training of leaders" (44). Coles answers the objection by noting the Bible does not call for a diploma or a degree from a seminary. Instead, Coles noted, based on 2 Timothy 2:2, "The apostle Paul described his training model as easily reproducible to multiple generations."

A theological treatment of movements and a development of movement missiology is presented in chapters six to ten by contributors David Lim, Craig Ott, Trevor Larsen, Michael T. Cooper, and James Lucas. Ott, professor of mission and intercultural studies at Trinity Evangelical Divinity School, identifies seven biblical dynamics of church planting movements: 1) Movements are a work of the triune God; 2) Movements are fueled by the Word of God, the gospel; 3) Movements are the result of evangelism that intentionally plants churches; 4) Movements empower ordinary believers to share their faith; 5) Movements are sustained by developing leaders; 6) Movements can expect to face opposition; and 7) Movements should be linked with the larger body of Christ (104-110).

In the chapters on "Biblical Dynamics of Movements," Steve Addison considers why movements rise and fall. Addison notes that the degree to which a movement stays anchored to Jesus Christ will determine its growth and sustainability. Pam Arlund and Regina Foard, in their chapter "From Her Perspective: Women and Multiplication Movements," call for an increased role and voice for women in mission movements and movement leadership.

In chapter thirteen, Paul Kuivinen offers a fascinating treatment of music and missions in his contribution, "How Ethnodoxology Drives Movements." Kuivinen documents how movement leaders working to reach UPGs are experiencing amazing breakthroughs as the people are learning the Scriptures through songs, melodies, and harmonies using their voices and indigenous musical instruments in creative and exciting ways. Such new approaches are making monumental impacts on how the gospel is spreading in regions that previously were hindered due to Western imports of songs and hymns by missionaries that did not resonate with the peoples in their cultures.

Frank Preston, in chapter fourteen, "Media to Movements: A Church Planting Fusion," explores how multimedia and online churches are helping to expand movements, especially during a time in which social media has exploded and in the context of the COVID-19 pandemic when people have been so socially isolated. Preston discusses how social media is helping to identify religious seekers and POPS (or "persons of peace") who are open to change and the gospel (214).

Bradley Cocanower and Joao Mordomo discuss movement work among people from the Global South who are in the Global North due to war, migration, or those seeking political asylum in their chapter, "Terra Nova: Opportunities and Challenges of Movement Work in Diaspora Contexts." Physical needs, financial needs, legal needs, language learning and culture adjustment needs, social connection and friendship needs, and counseling needs for people suffering the ravages of war, can all be daunting and overwhelming to refugees.

In chapters sixteen to eighteen, case studies describe and document tens of thousands of people coming to faith in Jesus Christ among Muslims in East Africa, Hindus in India, and Buddhists in Thailand. In chapter nineteen, Rania Mostofi and Patrick Brittenden ask, "How can we best participate in and work with the work of the Spirit so that his wind continues blowing through to the second generation?" (278).

Emanuel Prinz offers an empirical study using qualitative and quantitative data for a profile of an effective movement leader or catalyst in chapter twenty. In chapter twenty-one, Eric and Laura Adam discuss the paradigm shift of their organization from a church planting group to an organization pursuing movement methods and movement thinking, praying, and planning. In the final chapter, Richard Grady addresses questions using a listening symposium from experienced global movement leaders representing five continents on the next steps to continue and mature the discourse on discipleship movements.

Motus Dei is a remarkable achievement as a resource and scholarly work both in its breadth and depth for cutting-edge missiological research. One of the greatest strengths of Motus Dei is that it brings together the collaborative insights of thirty-two contributors from African, Middle Eastern, European, Asian, and North American regions. The rich backgrounds and experiences of contributors such as Victor John of India, coauthor of The Bhojpuri Breakthrough: The Movement that Keeps Multiplying (2019); David Garrison, author of the groundbreaking books Church Planting Movements (2004), T4T: A Discipleship Revolution (2011), and A Wind in the House of Islam (2014); and Pam Arlund, author of The Pocket Guide to Church Planting (2010), Fruit to Harvest (2018), and Conversations on When Everything is Missions (2020); all bring a wealth of background, experiences, and insights to the conversation on movements.

Another strength of Farah's *Motus Dei* was the invitation to join the global conversation on movements. Farah invites readers with significant movement experience or interest to join the Motus Dei network by connecting with their team through http://motusdei.network.

Motus Dei raised important issues and questions for further missiological reflection and research. Some of the questions were: Are the observations from researchers in reported movements unique to their regions or common across movements? How can movements institutionalize and yet retain their movement DNA or identities? How will movements interact with the broader body of Christ and their societies? What will be the contextualized theologies of movements and their emerging ecclesiologies?

The purpose of this book was not "to satisfy academic curiosity, but rather to provoke inquiry related to how God is at work in our world" (19). Farah and the contributors to the project *Motus Dei* accomplished their collective goal. They described, defined, and documented contemporary mission movements using a multilevel and multidisciplinary approach involving theologians, missiologists, social scientists, and practitioners.

A few areas not explored in the book were movements from populations native to the Global North and Latin America. In addition, although China was mentioned briefly in chapter five, "How Movements Count," no detailed reports of movements in communist countries were discussed. How could movements be initiated in communist countries such as China, Cuba, and North Korea to reach millions with the gospel? The reviewer agrees with Alan Hirsch in his Afterword to *Motus Dei* when he wrote, "While I recognize that *Motus Dei* has been written by (and mostly for) reflective practitioners and missiologists operating in the Global South, there was little reflection on how their remarkable insights might impact Christian mission in distinctly Western and post-Christian contexts" (339). How might the contributions and conversations from *Motus Dei* be used to revitalize and begin a movement of God in the Global North and Latin America?

GREAT COMMISSION

RESEARCH JOURNAL
2022, Vol. 14(2) 171-175

Book Review

Turning Points in the Expansion of Christianity: From Pentecost to the Present

By Alice Ott
Baker Academic, 2021
298 pages
$28.99.

Reviewed by David Thiessen. David serves as the Executive Pastor at Mountain View Church in Fresno, California. He is a Doctor of Ministry Student in Church Growth at the Talbot School of Theology at Biola University.

Inspired by historian Mark Noll's 1997 book, *Turning Points: Decisive Moments in the History of Christianity*, Alice Ott[1], a professor of history at Trinity Evangelical Divinity School, has written a history of the expansion of Christianity "across geographical, cultural, ethnic and religious boundaries" (xv). The author's intentional use of the term "expansion" rather than "mission" is intended to separate the book from being labeled as another history of Western missionary efforts. The book is, consequently, global in scope, in addition to being historically comprehensive. The author seeks to make some distinct contributions by devoting 100 pages to the expansion of Christianity prior to the rise of

---

[1] The author is spouse of author Craig Ott, a co-author, with Gene Wilson, of the important church planting textbook, *Global Church Planting: Biblical Principles and Best Practices for Multiplication* (Grand Rapids, MI: Baker Academic, 2011).

Protestant mission and by considering two, often-overlooked turning points—the influence of British abolitionism on mission efforts in Africa and the role of imperialism in mission (xxi).

The author offers the following list of 12 key turning points:

- The Jerusalem Council (49)
- Patrick and the Conversion of Ireland (ca. 450)
- The East Syrian Mission to China (635)
- Boniface and the Oak of Thor (723)
- Jesuits and the Chinese Rites Controversy (1707)
- Zinzendorf and Moravian Missions (1732)
- William Carey and the Baptist Missionary Society (1792)
- British Abolitionism and Mission to Africa (1807)
- Henry Venn and Three-Self Theory (1841)
- The Scramble for Africa (1880)
- The Edinburgh World Missionary Conference (1910)
- The Lausanne Conference on World Evangelism and Majority World Missions (1974)

Each turning point is given a full chapter and each chapter begins with a focus on the specific turning point in view. This is followed by a broader, historical view of other developments related to the key turning point. Each chapter then returns to the specific turning point for a summary analysis. The book concludes with a brief but important chapter that highlights what the author identifies as important and recurring themes in the history of Christianity's expansion: mission theology, mission agents and structures, mission and culture, mission and state, and mission motivation and lifestyle.

Turning Points is academic in style, chock full of names, places, and dates. Each chapter includes sidebars with extensive quotations from relevant, primary sources. The author demonstrates a command of an astonishingly wide range of historical detail and is able to connect related historical events extremely well. For example, in chapter two the author describes how seventh century monks from east Syria, led by a bishop named Alopen, traveled some 2500 miles to spread the gospel in China (42). They encountered a miraculously sympathetic emperor named Taizong, of the Tang dynasty, who granted them freedom to preach the gospel message (46). This became a turning point in the expansion of Christianity as it represented "the high point and culmination of the early and remarkable mission enterprise of the Church of the East" (63). The details of this relatively obscure chapter in the history of Christian mission are further enhanced with sidebars featuring quotations from the Nestorian Stele, a portion of an Ascension Day sermon by the Persian poet Narsai, and an excerpt from a seventh century theological treatise addressing monotheism.

The book also sheds light on how the expansion of Christianity intersected with other global events — a perspective that other histories can overlook. For instance, the author identifies the abolition of slavery in Africa as being a turning point in mission. While describing the shift in missional focus among Christians towards the African continent that coalesced during the late 1700s, the author notes that it was unique in two ways:

> First...the focus on Africa was intimately linked with a desire to make national reparation for the collective sin of complicity with slavery; and second, it was joined with a clear humanitarian agenda to root out all remaining vestiges of slavery in Africa. In these ways, British abolitionism and the resultant mission to Africa was a turning point in the expansion of Christianity. (163)

Over time, missionaries saw that replacing slavery with legitimate forms of commerce was the most effective means for its eradication and the three C's — Christianity, civilization, and commerce — became one of the earliest expressions of a more holistic approach to the expansion of Christianity (172, 175).

A third strength of the book is its important conclusions section where the author brings various mission-related themes together. Of particular importance is the theological foundation for mission. The author demonstrates again and again, that without adequate theological motivation, mission either does not get off the ground, or is quickly abandoned in the face of inevitable resistance and hardship. The author notes the importance of St. Patrick's recognition of Matthew 28 as a motivating call to disciple all the nations, even those beyond the Roman empire (20), the various doctrinal beliefs of the Reformation era that muted missional activity (114), the importance of the Moravians abandonment of 'first fruits' theology — expecting only a sprinkling of Gentile converts in favor of focusing on Jewish converts — for their continuing missional effectiveness (127), the refutation by William Carey and Andrew Fuller of the anti-missionary implications of hyper-Calvinism (139) and the drift of liberal, mainline churches away from the Gospel message in the 20th century (251).

To her five themes listed above, perhaps the author could have added a sixth theme of significance, namely, the miraculous timing orchestrated by the Holy Spirit. This timing is on display at various points in the history of the expansion of Christianity, including the remarkable openness of the Hawaiian people to the gospel message in 1820, owing to their very recent — just four months earlier! — repudiation of their centuries old traditional religion, knows as the kapu (Hawaiian for "taboo") system (153). Presumably the author would agree that the Holy Spirit's remarkable work of creating open doors to further the spread of the good news is at the heart of every turning point in Christianity's expansion.

Because of its academic style, sometimes obscure themes, and a somewhat complex chapter structure, *Turning Points* is no easy read. It occasionally gets bogged down in too much detail regarding names, places, and dates. A more generous use of footnotes might have improved the flow of the narrative. This is less of a weakness, given the academic goals of the book, and more of a warning for the casual reader.

A more significant critique is that at times it does not seem that the author is able to convincingly argue that the chosen turning point is indeed a decisive moment in the expansion of Christianity. For instance, in chapter ten the author asserts that "The Scramble for Africa"— a term used to describe "the rapid political partition, conquest, and colonialization of the African continent by European powers during the high imperialist era, circa 1880 to 1914"— was a turning point in the expansion of Christianity (208). But the chapter seems more of an exploration of the complex relationship between imperialism and missionaries on the field. The relationship was varied with some missionaries collaborating with imperialistic aims, and others resisting. So, while the expansion of Christianity certainly has had a complex relationship with colonialism, it is unclear how the historical events examined constitute an actual turning point.

Finally, any book of this type is inherently subjective and open to dispute regarding the choice of turning points. The list of possible turning points is endless, and the ranking of turning points in terms of importance is a hornet's nest. For instance, one perspective could insist that the rise of Pentecostalism impacted mission like nothing else, and that it represents a vital turning point. Or another viewpoint might emphasize the role of revivals in mission as being fundamental. Nevertheless, the list chosen here is worthy of serious consideration and the focus on lesser-known turning points and non-Protestant turning points does make this book's perspective unique. It remains an important historical contribution to the understanding of how Christianity has expanded and should be read widely.

Turning Points represents a remarkable combination of wide-ranging observations regarding mission coupled with an extraordinary grasp of primary resources. It makes a unique contribution to our understanding of the expansion of Christianity, highlighting many obscure events and saints whose contribution to Christian mission should not be forgotten. More importantly, it brings to life the truth that, "This same Good News that came to you is going out all over the world. It is bearing fruit everywhere by changed lives" (Colossians 1:6, NLT).

2023 Great Commission Research Network National Conference

INNOVATIONS
IN EVANGELISM
Faith Sharing for Ordinary People

March 6-7, 2023 • Orlando, Florida

This year's conference will be one of the Pre-Conferences at Exponential (Mar 7-9, 2023), a large conference focused on church multiplication (exponential.org). The conference is held at First Baptist Church of Orlando. Information on hotels can be found on Exponential's website.

The price for both the Great Commission Research Network (GCRN) Conference and Exponential is $158. Please register for both at greatcommissionresearch.com/conference

The GCRN conference begins on Monday, March 6, at 1:00pm and ends Tuesday, March 7, at Noon, after which the Exponential conference begins and continues through Thursday.

If you are interested in presenting research, please email a 100-200 word summary of your proposed presentation to Jay Moon, President of the GCRN, at jay.moon@asburyseminary.edu. Proposals will be accepted based on quality of research, relevance to the theme of the conference, and potential for application in local churches.

GREAT COMMISSION RESEARCH NETWORK

(formerly: The American Society for Church Growth)

OFFICERS

President:
Dr. Jay Moon
Professor of Church Planting and Evangelism
Asbury Theological Seminary
Email: jay.moon@asburyseminary.edu

First Vice President:
Dr. Brad Ransom
Chief Training Officer
Director of Church Planting
Free Will Baptist North American Ministries
Email: brad@nafwb.org

Treasurer:
Ben Penfold
Chief Executive Officer
Penfold & Company

GREAT COMMISSION RESEARCH NETWORK
greatcommissionresearch.com

MEMBERSHIP

What is the Great Commission Research Network?
The Great Commission Research Network (GCRN) is a worldwide and professional association of Christian leaders whose ministry activities have been influenced by the basic and key principles of church growth as originally developed by the late Donald McGavran. Founded by renowned missiologists George G. Hunter III and C. Peter Wagner, the GCRN has expanded into an affiliation of church leaders who share research, examine case studies, dialogue with cutting-edge leaders, and network with fellow church professionals who are committed to helping local churches expand the kingdom through disciple-making.

Who Can Join the GCRN?
GCRN membership is open to all who wish a professional affiliation with colleagues in the field. The membership includes theoreticians, such as professors of evangelism and missions, and practitioners, such as pastors, denominational executives, parachurch leaders, church planters, researchers, mission leaders, and consultants. Some members specialize in domestic or mono-cultural church growth, while others are cross-culturally oriented.

Why Join the GCRN?
The GCRN provides a forum for maximum interaction among leaders, ministries, and resources on the cutting edge of Great Commission research. The annual conference of the GCRN (typically held in March each year) offers the opportunity for research updates and information on new resources and developments, as well as fellowship and encouragement from colleagues in the field of church growth. Membership in the GCRN includes a subscription to the *Great Commission Research Journal* and a discount for the annual conference.

How Do I Join the GCRN?
For further information on membership and the annual conference, please visit greatcommissionresearch.com.

Membership Fees

- One-year regular membership (inside or outside USA) - $59
- One-year student/senior adult membership (inside or outside USA) - $39
- Three-year regular membership (inside or outside USA) - $177
- Three-year senior membership (inside or outside USA) - $117
- Membership includes a subscription to the *Great Commission Research Journal* which is in the process of transitioning to an electronic format.

GREAT COMMISSION RESEARCH NETWORK
AWARDS

Donald A. McGavran Award for Outstanding Leadership in Great Commission Research

Normally once each year, the GCRN gives this award to an individual for exemplary scholarship, intellect, and leadership in the research and dissemination of the principles of effective disciple-making as described by Donald A. McGavran. The award recipients to date:

Win Arn	1989	Charles Arn	2005
C. Peter Wagner	1990	John Vaughan	2006
Carl F. George	1991	Waldo Werning	2006
Wilbert S. McKinley	1992	Bob Whitesel	2007
Robert Logan	1993	Bill Easum	2009
Bill Sullivan	1994	Thom S. Rainer	2010
Elmer Towns	1994	Ed Stetzer	2012
Flavil R. Yeakley Jr.	1995	Nelson Searcy	2013
George G. Hunter III	1996	J. D. Payne	2014
Eddie Gibbs	1997	Alan McMahan	2015
Gary L. McIntosh	1998	Steve Wilkes	2016
Kent R. Hunter	1999	Art McPhee	2016
R. Daniel Reeves	2000	Mike Morris	2017
Ray Ellis	2002	Bill Day	2019
John Ellas	2003	Warren Bird	2022
Rick Warren	2004		

Win Arn Lifetime Achievement Award in Great Commission Research

This award is given to a person who has excelled in the field of American church growth over a long period of time. The award recipients to date:

Eddie Gibbs	2011	Gary McIntosh	2015
Elmer Towns	2012	Kent R. Hunter	2017
George G. Hunter III	2013	Carl George	2019
John Vaughan	2014	Charles Arn	2022

American Society for Church Growth/GCRN Past Presidents

C. Peter Wagner	1986	Ray W. Ellis	1999-00
George G. Hunter III	1987	Charles Van Engen	2001-02
Kent R. Hunter	1988	Charles Arn	2003-04
Elmer Towns	1989	Alan McMahan	2005-06
Eddie Gibbs	1990	Eric Baumgartner	2007-08
Bill Sullivan	1991	Bob Whitesel	2009-12
Carl F. George	1992	Steve Wilkes	2013-14
Flavil Yeakley Jr.	1993	Mike Morris	2015-16
John Vaughan	1994	James Cho	2017-18
Gary L. McIntosh	1995-96	Gordon Penfold	2019-20
R. Daniel Reeves	1997-98		

GREAT COMMISSION RESEARCH NETWORK
SUBMISSIONS

The *Great Commission Research Journal* publishes both peer-reviewed articles reporting original research and reviews of recent books relevant to evangelism and disciple making.

The scope of the journal includes research focusing on evangelism, church planting, church growth, spiritual formation, church renewal, worship, or missions. Articles come from both members and non-members of the Great Commission Research Network and are generally unsolicited submissions, which are welcomed and will be considered for peer-review. There is no charge for submission or publication.

ARTICLES

All submissions should be emailed to the editor, David R. Dunaetz at ddunaetz@apu.edu.

Peer Review Process

Only the highest quality submissions presenting original research within the scope of the journal will be chosen for publication. To ensure this, all articles will go through a peer review process. Articles deemed by the editor to have potential for publication will be sent to reviewers (members of the editorial board or other reviewers with the needed expertise) for their recommendation. Upon receiving the reviewers' recommendations, the author will be notified that the submission was either rejected, that the submission has potential but needs to be significantly revised and resubmitted, that the submission is conditionally accepted if the noted issues are addressed, or that the submission is accepted unconditionally.

Format

Papers should be APA formatted according to the 7th edition of the *Publication Manual of the American Psychological Association*. Submissions should include a cover page, be double-spaced in Times New Roman, and be between 3,000 and 7,000 words (approximately 10-22 pages) in .docx format. Contact the editor for exceptions to this word count.

In-text references should be in the form (Smith, 2020) or (Smith, 2020, p.100). At the end of the article should be a References section. No footnotes should be used. Minimize the use of endnotes. If endnotes are necessary, more than two or three are strongly discouraged; rather than using Microsoft Word's endnote tool, place them manually before the References section.

Include an abstract of approximately 100-150 words at the beginning of your text.

After the References section, include a short biography (approximately 30 words) for each author.

BOOK REVIEWS

The purpose of our book reviews is to direct the reader to books that contribute to the broader disciple making endeavors of the church. The review (500-2000 words) is to help potential readers understand how the book will contribute to their ministry, especially those in North America or which have a large cross-cultural base. The review should consist of a summary of the contents, an evaluation of the book, and a description of how the book is applicable to practitioners.

Before submitting a book review, please contact the book review editor Ken Nehrbass (krnehrbass@liberty.edu) to either propose a book to be reviewed or to ask if there is a book that needs to be reviewed.

COPYRIGHT

Copyrights on articles are held by the Great Commission Research Network with permission to republish given to the authors. Requests for permission to reproduce material from the journal, except for brief quotations in scholarly reviews and publications, should be directed to the general editor of the journal.

CONTACT INFORMATION

To submit an article or for general questions, contact:
Dr. David Dunaetz, ddunaetz@apu.edu

For questions about book reviews, contact:
Ken Nehrbass, krnehrbass@liberty.edu